Inclusion:
HOW TO

ESSENTIAL
CLASSROOM STRATEGIES

GARY BUNCH

INCLUSION PRESS

Canadian Cataloguing in Publication Data

Bunch, Gary Owen, 1938-
Inclusion: how to: essential classroom strategies

Includes bibliographical references.
ISBN 1-895418-42-9

1. Inclusive Education.   2. Handicapped children —   I. Title.

LC1200.B857 1999   371.9'046   C99-930489-5

Published by
Inclusion Press
24 Thome Crescent
Toronto, Ontario M6H 2S5
Canada

First Printing: 1999
Second Printing: 2002

Dedicated to

Kevin Hugh Finnegan
Celt, Musician, Inclusive Educator, Guide, Friend

Somebody said that it couldn't be done,
But he with a chuckle replied
That maybe it couldn't, but he would be one
Who wouldn't say so till he'd tried.

It Couldn't Be Done
Edgar Albert Guest

**With Appreciation
for Ideas and Feedback to**

Angela Valeo, Diana Massey, Rose Galati

and the
York University, Faculty of Education
Consecutive Teacher Preparation Program
Early Childhood Education Option Group of 1997 - 1998

Heather Alfenore, Laura Di Pietro, Jennifer Gonin, Fiona Gordon,
Stella Figueiredo, Lynda Green, Christina Guidotti, Darcia Isenor,
Tammy Johnston, Christine Kazlovski, Jeannette McCullough, Matthew Kean,
Paula Melo, Patrizia Olivieri, Tracey Parsons, Sussanah Parker,
Adriana Passarelli, Barbara Rodrigoe, Michelle Sack, Trisha Turner

CONTENTS

INCLUSION IN EDUCATION: PHILOSOPHY, NEED, AND BENEFIT

The teaching world is an amazing place at times. We have the most wondrous new technology, more powerful understanding of how students learn, and standardized testing programs aimed at separating the sheep from the goats. The list can go on and on. However, our teaching world is strange as well. For instance, a major activity within many educational systems is separating students, one from the other, on the basis of difference. It strikes us as strange that educators find so many students to be goats, emphasize that they are too different to learn as do their peers, remove them from the presence of their friends, and bus them out of their communities, all in pursuit of making them less different and assisting them to fit into society.

In this book the focus is on how to keep students together rather than arbitrarily and artificially separating them on the basis of difference in learning. But we could as easily be talking about present and past separation on the basis of race, gender, language, or culture. The school system has recognized that it is politically incorrect to separate students for these reasons, and has ceased segregating due to race, gender, and culture. Some students do continue to be separated on the basis of needing to learn the language of a new country, but only for a relatively short length of time. It is only in the instance of disability that some students remain segregated for their entire school careers, who are labeled for life. Educators offer many reasons for this segregation, all of them carrying negative connotations about the students.

We prefer not to dwell on these negative things. Yes, they exist. Yes, they represent barriers to acceptance. Yes, those who believe children learn best in the company of other learners in their community struggle against these facts with every fibre of their beings, and often are called on to do so. But, no. We will not accept that difference in learning ability should mean segregation of so many of our young people.

> **It simply is preferable and better to educate all students together. All the teachers teaching inclusively today prove that inclusion is possible and practical.**

There is much more value in regarding all the negatives which some educators come up with simply as proof of the need for a more positive approach to the strengths and needs of students with challenging needs. To begin with, we can stop labeling and rejecting them. Humans can love one another. Mother Teresa proved that every day. Humans can fight successfully for one another. Martin Luther King trumpeted this reality to his dying day. Humans can bend their every thought to bringing social justice to the rejected, demeaned, and isolated. Mothers and fathers, sisters and brothers, nurses, doctors, and tradespeople, and so many others prove that in their daily lives. Not least in this list are teachers who recognize the right of every child to be in the company of other children in the regular classrooms of our community schools.

As John Fitzgerald Kennedy said:

If we cannot end now our differences, at least we can make the world safe for diversity.

There is a need to include each other in our lives, loves, homes, schools, communities, and hearts. That need roars forth louder than all the distressing dynamics noted earlier.

Inclusion, true inclusion of all, will wipe segregation from the face of the earth. We teachers can begin by wiping it out of the worlds of the children we teach.

A Little Philosophy

Philosophy is a big word isn't it? It sounds so impressive. It sort of scares most of us, because we don't think we have a philosophy. We simply live our lives the way we live them. We don't think in philosophical terms.

INCLUSION: HOW TO

WELL, WE HAVE GOOD NEWS FOR YOU!

Philosophy is just a fancy word for a simple thing. We mustn't allow all those professors, and religious experts, and politicians, and other know-it-alls to scare us into believing that we don't have a philosophy of life. They all have their philosophies. We teachers aren't excluded in this regard. We do, too.

If you look in the dictionary, you will see that one of the meanings of philosophy is "a system of principles for guidance in practical affairs". Your philosophy is your own set of rules for how you live your teaching life. You can have a philosophy that says some children are better than others, and that they should keep to their own place in life. You know that philosophy.

- The "Children should be seen, but not heard" philosophy.
- The "Not in my backyard" philosophy.
- The "Lock them up and throw away the key" philosophy.
- The "Put them in special classes" philosophy.
- The "Educate the best and forget the rest" philosophy.

On the other hand, you can have a:

- **"We may all be different, but we are all more similar than different" philosophy.**
- **A "We all have gifts to give" philosophy.**
- **A "Let's get together and make the world a better place" philosophy.**
- **A "Do unto children what you would have others do unto your children" philosophy.**

WHICH DO YOU PREFER?

Meyer Shevin is a poet. He is a poet and many other things, as we all are more than the convenient pigeon holes into which others place us. Meyer sometimes writes about the way people think about themselves and others. One of his poems appears on the next page.

What Meyer is doing is laying out two philosophical approaches to our relationship to people whom we regard as different in some way. He is laying out two systems of "principles for guidance in practical affairs". Meyer is asking the great philosophical question:

HOW DO WE LIVE *WITH* ONE ANOTHER?

That is the question asked in this book as well. We ask it specifically with regard to the relationship of teacher and learner.

Our basic response, and that of many of our teacher colleagues, to the question "How do we live **WITH** one another?" is a single word.

What does this word mean for us? It means that all children have the right to be together in the community of the regular classroom. It says that all children have the right to go to the same school attended by their brothers, sisters, and neighbourhood friends. It says that placement in an educational program should depend on the needs of individual children for a natural environment, and not on some form of quasi-medical diagnosis or psychological measurement.

Language of Us/Them

We like things.
They fixate on objects.

We try to make friends.
They display attention thinking behavior.

We take breaks.
They display off task behavior.

We stand up for ourselves.
They are non-compliant.

We have hobbies.
They self-stim.

We choose our friends wisely.
They display poor peer socialization.

We persevere.
They perseverate.

We love people.
They have dependencies on people.

We go for a walk.
They run away.

We insist.
They tantrum.

We change our minds.
They are disoriented and have short attention spans.

We have talents.
They have splinter skills.

We are human.
They are ...?

Meyer Shevin

It says that all teachers can teach, and that all teachers can teach any child effectively at that child's level. It says that teachers need to be supported in their work, and it

> *Most of all, though, inclusion means that any child is welcome in regular classrooms, that there is a natural need for us all to belong within society, and that there are benefits to being included.*

says that part of the support system comes from family, friends, and peers (Bunch, 1989).

A Great Need

"I want to be included"! This simple statement is being spoken, signed, facilitated, key-boarded, whispered, and shouted by people of all ages, shapes, sizes, colours, and cultures. Many are making the request for themselves while others are asking for their relatives or friends. It is a simple request and the answer is equally simple. Teachers know this simple answer and many are saying it to children with any type or degree of challenge to their learning. **"Welcome to my classroom. Let's learn together"**.

Why, then, does this simple answer evoke such strong reactions in some educators? Why is welcoming students labeled "disabled" seen as an activity of the "radical" fringe. Caring for friends and families is not radical. Welcoming people who differ by race or gender is not revolutionary. These are normal everyday activities, even if they may be challenging in some respect, or a change from what we have done in the past.

We believe that the inclusion issue cuts directly to the core of our values and beliefs as teachers. Inclusion seems so simple, so full of common sense, so obviously beneficial. Yet it sets off fireworks in the souls of those involved. For those who practice inclusion, the fireworks light up from seeing the joy which accompanies bringing all students together. For those who resist inclusion, the fireworks come from seeing regular education being offered to students who are not seen as rightful members of a regular classroom.

But inclusion is <u>NOT</u> about placing a child with a disability in a classroom or school.

INCLUSION: HOW TO

We all have seen enough children who are placed physically in a classroom, but who are never included. Placement is only a tiny piece of the puzzle. Rather, inclusion is about how we deal with diversity, how we deal with difference, how we deal with human rights.

How else can we explain the emotions unleashed by the presence of a little child in a wheelchair or the presence of a child with Down Syndrome in a local school in Canada, or the US, or the UK, or any other country? Why do so many apparently "normal" educators, whose profession it is to teach children, lose their composure with the mere mention of including a child with low scores on some standardized test, or one whose behaviour is not the same as that of most children? We hypothesize that the fear is of change, change to the way we do things, change to the way we understand our world to operate. It seems to us that someone once said:

> **THE ONLY THING WE HAVE TO FEAR IS FEAR ITSELF.**

This someone was Franklin Delano Roosevelt in his first inaugural address; a great leader, a great teacher of society, and a person who used a wheelchair.

True, fear suggests that there is danger. Change may be the danger many teachers see. However, in danger there is also opportunity for growth. Thus, schools and communities, teachers and citizens, who face their fears by **WELCOMING ALL CHILDREN** instantly create the climate for a new kind of environment. Inclusion becomes an opportunity and a catalyst for building a better, more humane, and democratic system.

Inclusion does not mean we are all the same.

Inclusion does not mean we all agree.

Shared Benefit
Rather, inclusion celebrates our diversity and difference with respect and gratitude. The greater our diversity, the richer our capacity to create new visions.

Inclusion is a teacher's antidote to racism, sexism, and abilism because it welcomes those differences and celebrates them as capacities rather than deficiencies. Inclusion is a farce when it means only "white, bright, and middle class". Inclusion means all together accepting and supporting one another.

A child or adult with a disability is a symbolic personal test through which we teachers face our feelings about differences head on. Inclusion is about how we relate to people who look, act, or think differently than do so-called "ordinary" people. Inclusion can be deeply disturbing, for it challenges our unexamined notions of what "ordinary" and "normal" really mean. Our hidden values are paraded before us in action and reaction. Some of what we see is discomforting. The questions become very personal.

- **How would I feel if I were unable to walk, talk, or move?**

- **How would I feel if I had a child who was disabled?**

- **How would I feel if I were disabled in an accident?**

- **How do I feel about myself?**

This is what Hahn (1988) calls existential anxiety. We fear that we will be like those with disabilities and therefore we reject them. We don't give them a chance. But if we do accept them and get to know them, we discover that a person with a disability is simply a person. Giving all students a chance is most especially vital to teachers who meet all the young of every community and whose job it is to assist them to develop positively. We must admit, meet, and defeat our own fears, if we are to understand the fears of our students and their parents, and if we are to help them to meet their fears and defeat them.

Research and practice are clear. Inclusion is both possible and practical. It is academically and socially stronger for all students than are other educational solutions to disability (see Bunch

& Valeo, 1997). Teachers all over the world know from personal experience that they can teach inclusively without burning out, and without lowering standards. <u>We know that it is better for all students to learn together and that teachers can create an inclusive environment.</u>

This book is written to give you some ideas of how inclusive education may be undertaken. Several major guidelines and strategies are suggested.

But in the end, you will be an inclusive educator because you believe that all children are learners and that you are their teacher.

> **You learn to talk by talking.**
>
> **You learn to read by reading.**
>
> **You learn to write by writing.**
>
> **You learn to include by including.**

Gary Bunch, Marsha Forest, & Jack Pearpoint

CLASSROOM CULTURE

The inclusive classroom is a classroom which has accepted the right of any student to participate with all others in the process of learning. Difference in race, ethnicity, and gender do not lessen that right. Neither does difference in ability. All learners are accepted as members of the classroom community as equal participants within their abilities and needs.

For the teacher this means the planning and implementation of practices and strategies designed to foster a classroom culture which reflects certain principles.

- **All children have a right to a place in the regular classroom.**

- **All children have individual abilities and needs which should be recognized.**

- **All children are learners.**

- **Teachers and students are colleagues in the act of learning.**

Fortunately, all teachers know how to foster a positive learning environment in which these principles are featured. If there is one thing that teachers are really good at, it is knowing how to design and implement effective learning environments for a wide range of students. Some teachers may decide, for personal and/or professional reasons, not to accept and enact these principles, but we all know them. And we know they produce good education. A glimpse at some basic strategies and ideas will serve to remind us of our knowledge.

$$\boxed{\textit{STRATEGIES}}$$

Developing a Classroom Community

The culture of the classroom is developed by the teacher and students. The teacher can do much to encourage positive relationships among all children: the key is acceptance of all for their unique selves, and support of all in the tasks and activities of learning. What are some of the major strategies?

$$\boxed{\textit{Keeping Everyone Informed}}$$

A.   Many inclusive classrooms hold a meeting at the beginning of each week to share information, discuss what remains to be done from the previous week, explore what this week's work will include, note any points regarding mutual support needs, and review special events in class or school. Such meetings permit students to be involved in decision-making, recognize the social and community basis of learning, and focus both on work to be undertaken and individual abilities and needs.

Use a consistent opening format with a song or quiet game-type activity to obtain attention and participation. This gives those with challenges in getting ready and focusing a chance to prepare. Starting the day with a familiar and comfortable routine helps others as well.

Put in place a method of recognizing one speaker at a time. A speaker's baton can be passed to the next speaker while discussion finishes on the previous topic. Some students need to see concrete evidence of turn-taking in order to reduce habits of just talking out. Other students will have time to reorient to a new speaker visually and/or auditorily.

INCLUSION: HOW TO

B.   Use the same strategies for an end-of-the-week meeting.

C.   Put the day's agenda up each morning (using words, illustrations, or other symbols) to remind all of what will occur as the day goes on. Those with memory needs will find this helpful. Others who need assurance will be reminded of the routine of the day.

D.   Work out an agreed on system for shifting from one activity to another. Consider appointing a student as the leader in getting the attention of peers and spread this privilege morning and afternoon among all students, including those who have challenge in ending activities or paying attention.

E.   Create small teams of students to coordinate classroom activities of a routine nature. Among such activities could be passing out books or paper, setting out art supplies, preparing materials for a peer with challenges, or setting up the VCR or tape player. Involve all students in such helping activities.

F.   Reserve a chalkboard space for building up a list of topics for the next week's opening and closing meetings. Items can be listed by any class member. All can see the topics and have a chance to prepare their thoughts or ask for focus on any issue of interest to them.

G.   _____

_____

H.   _____

_____

I.

_____

_____

J.

_____

_____

| Joint Decision-Making |

Democracy in action is a desired characteristic of the inclusive classroom. We need to recognize that the teacher has ultimate responsibility for all activities, but that it is a positive teaching strategy to share responsibility with students as often as possible. Sometimes it is good even to share responsibility with those students whose ability to accept responsibility you might question.

A. Set up a system in which students can volunteer to work on activities or events. An example would be the timing and themes of class parties. Another would be working as a peer tutor. A third would be inviting a guest speaker or challenging another class to raise money to donate to a preferred cause.

B. Vote for class president, student council representatives, or other position.

C. Involve students in determining the timetable. It is a good idea to let the students know the curriculum flexibility and restrictions you have as a teacher so that they can look at the task in an informed fashion. Let students contribute to curricular ideas for peers.

D. Open up a role for all students in setting class guidelines.

E. _____

_____

F. _____

_____

G. _____

_____

H. _____

_____

Forging a Community

The fundamental premise of an inclusive classroom is that it is a community from which no one is excluded and in which everyone is recognized for individual abilities and needs. Some teachers have devised specific ways to build community among their students. You can use these, design your own, get your students to help you with more, and rely on your colleagues to come up with even more. And don't forget the parents. The whole community is your resource.

Issues of disability can form part of this effort, but the idea of community goes far beyond this one area. There is no reason why your class or school community cannot extend positive actions related to disability to other areas such as race, ethnicity, age, immigration, and a great deal more determined by local needs.

A. Design a class T shirt or cap. Individual motto's, colours, or illustrations are possible. Run a contest with your students as judges. Cost may be met by parents, or by fundraising strategies.

B.   Adopt a class song, poem, or motto. Use something emphasizing acceptance, unity, a positive view, triumph over adversity. Such supports motivate and sustain class members, and teachers.

C.   Develop a plan for the class to contribute to the school or to the general community. Work with your students, parents, and colleagues.

- A monthly clean-up of the school grounds.
- A visit to a local senior citizens' setting to share songs, poems, and games.
- Write to community officials and individual citizens in recognition of a positive action or recommending a desired positive action affecting the community.
- _____

   _____

- _____

   _____

- _____

   _____

D.   _____

   _____

INCLUSION: HOW TO

E. _____

_____

F. _____

_____

G. _____

_____

Diversifying the Classroom

An inclusive classroom signals that it is diverse in many ways. Some of these are described under other headings, but there are some with particular effect on classroom culture that you might think about here. As informed educators we know these, but, at times, they appear to escape our notice. They should, however, be as present in our classrooms as are our students and ourselves. As this discussion focuses on diversity in terms of ability, the following suggestions use disability as a context. There is no reason that these ideas, and dozens of others, cannot be extended to other areas of diversity. Classrooms can be diversified in many small and subtle ways, as well in the larger, more easily identified ways.

    A.   Display student work. Teachers must resist the temptation, or the suggestions of others, that whatever work goes up should be correct and conventionally attractive. Due to the fact that an inclusive classroom includes students of differing ability levels, quite different levels of correctness and style will result from classroom activities. The work of all students should be displayed, not just the work of students who produce what is considered the "best". Your students will be a wonderful resource in working out ways to display non-

-17-

traditional products.

B.   Most classrooms contain a variety of reading materials. Among these materials should be those that recognize the presence of individuals with disabilities in the community. There is an increasing amount of children's literature which recognizes those with disabilities in positive and community oriented ways. In fact, I prepared such a resource myself (see Bunch, 1995).

C.   Often students with challenges, particularly those with high levels of challenge, are seated on the fringes of the classroom for convenience of getting to them easily to offer assistance, or due to the specialized equipment they may need. The seating plan can marginalize students or it can be designed to make them a part of the group. Inclusion may call for a little inconvenience and creative thought when determining who sits where.

D.   Many teachers involve students in keeping the classroom running: collecting books, putting things away, running messages, passing out papers. Those with inclusive philosophies ensure that all students share these responsibilities. Sometimes, however, certain students are excluded from specific responsibilities due to the nature of some challenging condition. For instance, a student who is known to "take off" at times, may not be included in running messages to the office or other parts of the school. Could there be a way to handle this situation so that all students are involved over time? If you are stuck, ask the students how to include the one you think may encounter difficulty in handling the task.

E. _____

_____

F. _____

_____

G. _____

_____

H. _____

_____

Recognizing Diversity with Honesty

Our society has developed a pattern of not dealing directly with disability. It makes us uneasy and we don't know how to respond to those who have disabilities. As we know, one of the major responses of the educational system has been to create a segregated system of special classes, special teachers, and special almost everything else. Inclusion is based on acceptance of the fact that it is normal for some members of the community to be disabled. There is no reason for putting them aside simply because their needs and the challenges of addressing them require us to think about how we can include them.

Teachers can promote acceptance and eliminate uneasiness by simple honesty. Honesty will promote a positive classroom climate. It is no secret to the other students that Nadira or Glenn has a disability. It is no secret to Nadira or Glenn either. Honest acceptance of such facts as part of the classroom culture by the teacher from day one will do much to set a positive model for the students, and for other teachers.

A. Deal as directly with students with challenging needs regarding work and behavioural expectations as you would with any other student. Of course, your expectations will differ from student to student depending on the level of their abilities, their individual personalities, and, for those with disabilities, the degree of their challenges. But deal with them simply as a student from whom you expect certain things.

B. When you find that your expectations must vary markedly, tell all students what you are doing and why. The great majority of students will cooperate with you when they understand what is happening. They know that it is unfair to treat everyone exactly alike.

C. Consider having the student in question, a family member, or other knowledgeable person explain the nature of a particular challenge. Of particular value in this strategy are community members with disabilities themselves. As with most things, what has been explained and given a chance to become familiar loses its mysteriousness and gains acceptance.

D. Admit to your students that sometimes you may be challenged in devising ways to include all students in participation. They will come to your assistance and share the load with you within their capacities. Care must be taken not to overburden the students, but you can check this possibility with a little thought. Your students, including those with some type of challenge to their learning, will appreciate you even more for your honesty.

E. _____

_____

F. _____

_____

G. _____

_____

H. _____

_____

Being Fair, Not Charitable

One danger of including students with challenges in all classrooms is that a culture of charity will result. A student with a disability is not in a regular classroom as an act of charity. He/she is there because that is where other children are, because that is the best site for learning, and because that is where the children of the community come together most frequently. Simply being aware of the danger of a culture of charity will go a long way toward helping you to avoid it. Some of the ideas in this material will be helpful as well, as will be the ideas of your students, their parents, and your colleagues. A few specific ideas are presented here.

    A.   Let your students know the danger of a charitable approach and how it may demean those with disabilities. Work with them to realize that responding to people according to their needs is simple equity and justice and not something to be given to some like a gift. There are resources (people, videos, books, magazines) in your community which will assist you in this area.

B.   Consider strategies to recognize and respond to the needs of all students equitably. For instance, when someone is away ill, call them or e mail them or write to them. When any student finds work overly challenging, respond with flexibility, even for the most able or for those with the greatest degree of challenge.

C.   Involve all your students, including those with challenging needs, in helping each other. Some students will have specific skills from which others will benefit. Some may simply need someone to hold their coat for a moment. It is the act of helping that is important, not whether the help is large or small.

D.   Make a point of including stories and information about people who work for and with others without thought of praise or reward. Examples would be police officers, medical personnel, fire fighters, social workers, advocacy organizations, community coaches, and even teachers and parents. A culture of one supporting the other can be part of your classroom.

E.   Model rejection of certain behaviours as inappropriate, while maintaining acceptance of the individual. Some students have short fuses due to the nature of their challenges. Some seek attention due to insecurity. You know the variety of inappropriate behaviours students, and sometimes adults, can show. Inappropriate behaviour should be dealt with quickly within the regular rules of the classroom, whether or not a student has a disability. However, as mentioned earlier, it is no secret to anyone that a particular student may have a challenging condition which results in more frequent inappropriate behaviour than another student. The same applies to students who may not be feeling well, those who do not have a good breakfast, or those with a troubled home environment. You may need to accept more from one student than from another in acting to meet individual needs. You will find that all students accept differential tasks and expectations, if you let them know what you are doing and why. Nothing defeats negative reactions as effectively as do openness and honesty.

F. _____

_____

G. _____

_____

H. _____

_____

I. _____

_____

FINAL THOUGHTS

There is absolutely no doubt but that you will develop a classroom culture. Part of that culture will grow from how much you contribute of yourself. Part will depend on the degree to which you create a secure environment in which your students may contribute. I suggest that building the classroom culture be a joint venture, and that your role is one which creates opportunities for a developing community.

To this end, discussion in this chapter concentrates on outlining areas, such as Keeping Everyone Informed, Diversifying the Classroom, and Being Fair, Not Charitable, and related strategies which will lead to a classroom culture in which all learners are welcome, irrespective of differences. Play your role well in this and your students will respond now and in their adult future.

A CHALLENGE FOR YOU

In 15 words or less, describe the culture of your classroom.

_____

_____

_____

_____

_____

THE ACCESSIBLE CURRICULUM

Every teacher knows what "curriculum" means in the usual sense. It is the program of studies laid down by a school or other authority for an area of learning.

- ✔ It may refer to what is studied in math, say, for one year. (E.g. the Grade four math curriculum)

- ✔ It may refer to math as studied over a number of years at continually increasing levels of sophistication. (E.g. the elementary school math curriculum)

The view of curriculum as a continuous process of learning in any area is preferred for inclusive classrooms.

This view gives more power to the teacher for the control of whatever aspect of the curriculum is being studied, and gives more opportunity for children to study at the level of the curriculum appropriate to their needs. The teacher who believes that teaching starts with the needs of the child, and that the curriculum should be interpreted flexibly to meet those needs is a teacher who can function inclusively. It is this teacher who realizes that expecting a child to fit into a set curriculum at any grade is a prescription for frustration for the teacher and failure for the child.

THE CURRICULUM IS NOT OUR MASTER. IT IS OUR SERVANT IN EDUCATION.

The inclusive teacher is a student oriented professional who:

☺   **Knows the student is more important than the curriculum.**

☺   **Knows that differences among students are to be valued.**

☺   **Knows every student is a learner.**

☺   **Knows children learn better together than apart.**

☺   **Knows the teacher can control the curriculum to the benefit of the student.**

☺   **Knows the effort is worth the prize of a child's learning.**

FUNDAMENTAL QUESTIONS FOR SUCCESSFUL TEACHING

Ask yourself four simple but fundamental questions as you plan your teaching for any student. Reflecting on these questions, and using them as guides, can assist you in working with all your students and ease the challenges of diverse ranges of ability.

1. What is the essential knowledge to be gained?

Which is more essential when studying the discovery of America?

■   That people crossed the ocean in fragile ships from the old world and found the new world?

■   That Columbus' ships were the Nina, Pinta, and Santa Maria?

There are essential points and points of detail and elaboration in any area. It is interesting, and may win you a point in a trivia contest, to know the names of Columbus' ships. But is it simply an elaboration to the essential fact of the finding of the new world?

Most learners are quite capable of mastering the essential facts and in adding to these a number of such details. Some will delve into details and elaborations of the essential facts and master them all, because that is the level and character of their ability. Others may find it sufficiently challenging to master only the essentials.

> **It is the essential information which is the focus of any lesson and of any act of learning. Determine the essentials and the elaborations of any lesson for your benefit and that of your students.**

2. How do my students learn best?

We know that different children have different learning styles. Fortunately, the majority can learn under a variety of instructional approaches with relative ease. Others benefit most from an approach which is chosen to fit their personal learning styles. It is fortunate also that most teachers can determine basic learning needs and also possess some understanding of learning needs and styles. If you need a refresher or some basic information on altering your classroom environment so that all students may learn at their best, see the later discussion on this topic.

In general, I find it helpful to ask myself questions regarding how a student might learn more powerfully. The answers tend to become self evident once we think of the options available, and as long as we don't limit the possibilities. Most are not really tough to think of. It is actually doing the thinking that may be the toughest.

- If a student has a hearing impairment, is it best for the teacher to rely solely on verbal communication or to support verbal communication with visual stimuli such as print and pictures?

- If a student needs some type of movement to support learning, should all students be expected to always remain seated and still?

We are the teachers. We know the answers to such questions and to a great many more. Just as Helen Reddy proclaimed "I am woman", so we can state proudly "I am teacher". The inclusive philosophy simply says that if we remember to ask the fundamental question of how a student learns best, then we will be more insightful and effective in our teaching. We can bring our knowledge to bear to our advantage and that of our students.

> **Student-centered teaching is more than a concept. It is a practice that will benefit all your students. In essence, it is simply good teaching.**

3. What modifications to a lesson would permit more students to learn effectively in my classroom?

Teachers know how to modify. You have studied how to make your lessons meaningful and have made modifications time after time as you assessed your students' learning needs. To review and perhaps extend your knowledge, this manual is sprinkled with ideas for modifications and adaptations.

At this point, it is sufficient to look back at your responses to the first two fundamental questions. If you can differentiate the essentials from the details and elaborations of any topic, and if you think about how your students learn best, you will have gone a long way to developing appropriate modifications for any student, no matter what learning ability level he or she has.

INCLUSION: HOW TO

THE SECRET OF SUCCESSFUL MODIFICATION IS FLEXIBILITY.
VIEW THE CURRICULUM AS A PLIABLE GUIDE
WHICH MAY BE SHAPED TO THE NEEDS OF THE STUDENT.

For instance, verbal communication, particularly when supported by an appropriate hearing aid system, can do much for many hearing impaired students. However, routine use of an overhead projector, the chalkboard, or other method of presenting essential information visually also will help those with hearing impairment. A peer note-taker is a valuable support for the student who must focus on speechreading and finds note taking challenging. At times, an educational assistant or volunteer with sign language skills is valuable. These ideas and others are available through collaboration with resource teachers, peers, parents, and others. A number of these modifications to routine instruction will assist other students in the class as well. Good teaching tends to have effect across the entire class.

4. How will my students show what they have learned?

Teaching curriculum content does not end when you have presented your lesson. When your part is done, it is time to for your students to show you how well you have taught. Your success is determined by how well your students can demonstrate their learning.

What is the trick to testing your success? The answer is one that most teachers know, if they pause for reflection.

ASK STUDENTS TO RESPOND IN WAYS THEY CAN HANDLE.

＊Take Shalini as an example.

Shalini is eight years old. She is a pretty, slim girl of East Indian origin born here. Making friends, chatting, art, and dancing are among her strengths. Shalini has been challenged by print since she entered school, both in reading and in writing. At this time she has a sight vocabulary of almost 100 common words together with the names of friends and a few school terms. She reads simple stories well, as long as vocabulary has been pre-taught. She can print almost all her words, but syntax is slow in coming. She reads and prints numbers to 100.

Shalini's class is studying a unit on butterflies. This week the specific work includes reading a story about a butterfly emerging from the pupa and then imagining in writing what adventures the butterfly has.

During the lesson should the teacher:

> (a) ask Shalini to do exactly what the other students do?
>
> (b) exclude Shalini from the activity?
>
> (c) have a friend read the story to Shalini and then have Shalini imagine in writing what adventures the butterfly has?
>
> (d) have a friend read the butterfly story to Shalini and then have Shalini record her own story on a cassette?

I'll bet you chose (d), because you have the sense to realize that the other choices penalize Shalini in one way or another. You know that you obtain a clearer view of her learning ability by assessing her through her strengths than through her weaknesses. You could, also, pre-teach new vocabulary, or arrange to have a simplified version of the story prepared for Shalini and other students who might benefit from it, or have her do her story as a series of pictures, or give her pictures for her to put in story order, or .... The ideas are not that difficult to come by.

INCLUSION: HOW TO

Shalini has a variety of strengths. She also has some areas of need, most particularly those of reading and writing. If her teacher asked her to read to obtain information or to write to show that she has obtained information, Shalini would be put at a disadvantage. The teacher would be asking her to use her areas of challenge to learn, and to demonstrate that she has learned. But Shalini makes friends easily. Why not pair her with a friend who can read the story to her. She does not appear to have difficulties talking, judging by her enjoyment of chatting. Why not have her put her story about the butterfly on a cassette?

The same idea extends to students with other areas of challenge. As a teacher, one of your responsibilities is to strengthen areas of weakness and you must pay constant attention to strategies which will do so. One of your responsibilities also is to allow your students to show what they know without placing barriers in front of them. This is why I suggest that one of my four fundamental questions is "How will my students show their learning?". This is so important to students with challenges, and so unfair to them if not considered.

If you aren't certain about someone's strongest response style, why not ask? Students may not always know exactly what their strengths are, but often they will have ideas and they tend to benefit from being asked. If they are really uncertain, or if their degree of challenge interferes with a clear response, ask the other students or the parents, or ask a colleague. If you have adopted a collaborative approach, you do not have to do it all alone.

The central element in all four fundamental questions is that you have tried to go to where the student is in your teaching. If you do that, you will truly be the master of the curriculum, and your students will do better.

A simple form with the four fundamental questions and room to make some notes follows. It is most valuable when used to plan for a student with challenges. You will find that once you have used it a few times, the four questions will become automatic as guides to your planning. It will take hardly any time at all to include the needs of your student with challenges as you do your basic planning for your class.

FUNDAMENTAL QUESTIONS FOR LESSON PLANNING

TOPIC:_____

1. What is the essential knowledge to be gained?

_____

_____

_____

_____

_____

2. How will my students learn best in this lesson?

_____

_____

_____

_____

_____

3. What modifications to this lesson are necessary?

_____

_____

_____

_____

_____

4. How will my students show their learning?

_____

_____

_____

_____

_____

INCLUSION: HOW TO

DO I HAVE TO DO IT ALL ALONE?

This is a fair question. In answering it, it is useful to recall another fundamental which often is not emphasized enough in our professional development, nor often enough by the leaders in our schools.

Teaching & learning is a social affair.

Neither is possible without other people.

Your closest colleague in teaching is the learner. Without the learners, their involvement and their cooperation, you will be in for a frustrating time. Ideas for involving your students as active partners in defining and mastering the curriculum best for them will be found throughout this manual. Remember:

A: **You are surrounded by teaching colleagues with a wealth of ideas. You and your learners do not stand alone in dealing with the curriculum**. A resource teacher can advise you, suggest programming, teaching, and assessment strategies, and listen to your worries. Other regular class teachers can suggest ways to understand the curriculum and to approach it flexibly. You will benefit also from what they have tried, what didn't work for them, and what did work. They can be a tremendous resource to you, as you can be to them.

B: **Increasingly, there are knowledgeable people in the larger community around you to whom you can turn for advice.** The social service field has professional colleagues who have learned a great deal about child needs, strengths, and desires. Strategies they have developed for the curriculum of life outside the school may work inside it as well. Every community has resource people who work to include all children in the community in clubs, churches, synagogues, mosques, sports, and other areas. Try the Cubs, the Scouts, the Brownies, the Girl Guides, dance and music groups, religious instruction groups, and anyone else who may have gathered experiences in including people.

C: Do not forget the other students. They are a fantastic resource!

Your students possess understanding of individual needs and abilities. They have wonderfully creative ideas for putting across information. They have patience you can hardly imagine. They are natural risk takers. Often they don't know that something can't be done, so they go ahead and do it. More about peers in later pages, but do not underestimate their potential contribution.

D: Finally, and importantly, there are the parents.

They, together with you, know best how a particular child learns, what preferences exist, what times are best for what types of task, and many other things. Though the home may call for a curriculum differing in many ways from that of the school, its value cannot be questioned. It is the missing complementary half to your school and classroom. And the parents began dealing with their half long before you came on the scene. They deal with it before you start your teaching each day and after you stop for the day; they deal with it on weekends and holidays. They are a resource not to be ignored.

E.   _____

_____

INCLUSION: HOW TO

G. _____

_____

H. _____

_____

I. _____

_____

WRAP UP

The answer to "Do I have to do it alone?" is

collaborative teaching.

You have a great many colleagues available to support your work with any student. In some ways there are more available for support when students with challenging needs are involved. Reach out and ask them to work with you.

THEY WILL!!!!!!!

All of the above deals with making your curriculum accessible to all students at the level of their needs and abilities, making the curriculum accessible. This is really your job as a teacher. It can be challenging. It can be demanding. It does have varying levels of success. You may need to experiment and become a risk taker.

Taking charge of the curriculum and not permitting it to control you and your students is worth it in the returns you and your students will get.

THE ACCESSIBLE CURRICULUM

Student Centered

↕

Student Strengths and Needs

↕

Collaboration

↕

Focus on Essentials

↕

Modifications

↕

Reflective Practice

MAN IS A SOCIAL ANIMAL

Spinoza declared this as fact. Man is a social animal. And you know that Education is a social event. Our society has decided that children learn best when brought together in neighbourhood schools, placed together in age-appropriate groups, and guided by a knowledgeable teacher. Over the past years we have recognized that it is the right of students, regardless of race, ethnicity, or gender, to be together for their good and the good of society.

There is no reason to forget this when we think about students with some type of challenge to their learning. Inclusive educators believe that the social aspect of learning is so basic that all children of a community should be educated together in the regular classrooms of neighbourhood schools. Reasons for separating children are few and far between.

In this belief inclusive educators are supported by Piagetian theory which has given rise to much of our understanding of the discovery process of education and, particularly in recent years, to conflict resolution, Peace Keepers, and other such strategies in the area of behavioural challenges. **Vygotsky's** emphasis on the positive aspect of socialization on mental functioning and on social interaction to advance learning are supportive as well, and particularly attuned to inclusive teaching. A range of other theoretical positions, such as contact theory, which argues that people learn best about each other by being with each other, also support inclusion of all students in regular classrooms.

There is plenty of research available which proves that when students are educated together, their self-esteem and learning develop more than if they are separated (Bunch & Valeo, 1997). Bringing children together is simply good for them, even if differences exist. We know that the similarities we all share far outweigh any differences we might have. This goes both for students with challenging needs and for regular students.

Added to this is the knowledge of teachers that all children have a right to belong and that self-esteem is largely, if not completely, developed through routine contact with a diverse range of others. It is only when you are a part of the regular community, in constant contact with peers, walking the same hallways, enjoying the same activities, enduring the same disciplines, and doing all things together, that a sense of self as more similar to others than different can be developed. Inclusive educators recognize the truth of this. They focus on children, not on disabilities, in their professional determination to grant every student the greatest possible opportunity to achieve.

STRATEGIES

There are many challenges to the teacher in maintaining an inclusive classroom. Education is not a simple job. It is tough, often demanding, sometimes tiring. It is also a great joy. Here are some strategies which may assist you in creating a socially positive environment which will welcome all children to your classroom. Of course, other ideas may be obtained through collaboration with your teaching colleagues, professional development, reading, and access to technology. You may already know those which follow. They are simply samples from which you may extend with your own creativity and knowledge of your children.

✎**Classrooms should be designed for interaction**.

Seating plans which allow for small group and larger group activities, as well as individual learning, are encouraged. Related to this are the practices of collaboration, learning styles, and multiple intelligences addressed more fully in a later section. Remember to set up a plan which allows all equal access to any activity, but which does not place included students routinely on the edges of the group.

✎ **Group decision making is powerful.**

Class meetings, and the weekly opening meeting suggested earlier, are positive tools which develop social cohesion and can address particular problems and needs. Say a situation comes up where a few students are fooling around and disturbing others. You can set punishments. Or you can hold a five minute meeting in which students can review accepted classroom behaviour and discuss appropriate ways to maintain it. In this way you make the group responsible for their own behaviour. It may take a while to set up the routine, and it will not solve all the problems, but teachers find group decision making effective and valuable in advancing the social curriculum.

✏ Saying "Hello" to your students.

Did you ever attend a class where the teacher appeared not to recognize your existence, or the existence of another student, other than to give you work or note your deficiencies? This is an unfortunate fact in many classrooms for some students. They may be the unattractive, the too intelligent, the English as a second language student, the student with hearing loss. What did you feel like? What do they feel like? How should you try to make them feel?

As often as possible, be at the door when students enter in the morning, in the afternoon, or after recess. Say hello to them, ask them if they are feeling okay, comment on the weather. You do not have to reflect long to understand the value to all students of being recognized by the teacher. I think it is referred to as being a "model".

If you want to try out this strategy, there are a few things to consider. One is that you may feel it artificial to stand at the door and say "Hello" to a line of thirty students. You are right. It is. Try greeting a few each time, or stopping at someone's desk during the day for a personal word, or saying "Have a nice recess". You may not be able to cover every student, every day, but you will be able to cover everyone in a short time. If you can't remember whom you spoke to, a little checklist maintained in private, and taking up very little time, can be useful.

✏ **Being helpful to others.**

One characteristic of community is that people help each other. Teachers can encourage helpfulness by creating situations where help can be offered to all students.

For instance, students can assist each other by reminding each other of appointment times or how much time is left to finish a piece of work. Someone might need assistance pushing a wheelchair. Someone else might need help concentrating on a reading assignment. You can bring such opportunities to the attention of students and draw on volunteers to ensure that things are done as efficiently and as positively as possible. Be careful not to make helping a duty. A "duty" approach also brings with it the thought of reward, or perhaps of imposition. It might also foment a charitable attitude rather than a truly helping one. Some teachers create a "Volunteer Board" on which volunteers' names are listed. For any task that comes up, the next volunteer in line helps out. One benefit of this approach is that the volunteer receives some public recognition. Another is that you can monitor who is volunteering and try to find ways to encourage all to participate.

✏ **Asking for help.**

As well as developing opportunities for students to volunteer to assist others, it is possible to create opportunity for you and your students to ask for assistance. Somehow in our society we have made it sort of questionable to ask for help. That is one of the things that leads to a charitable view of helping someone, rather than simply the view that it is alright to help and just fine to need help at times. It often is the subtle things a teacher does with a class that have the greatest effect. Not all teaching need be direct. This is especially true of the social curriculum.

The idea of a "Request Board", similar to the Volunteer Board, is one that has worked for teachers. You and your students can make a variety of needs known by listing requests on the board. Requests such as "I need a red colour pencil to finish my picture", or "I can't read with Jenny today. Could anyone take over for me?" It is useful to let your students know that they can seek the assistance of others, just as they can volunteer assistance.

✏ Seeing the social side of lessons.

Educators tend to have a stronger attraction to the cognitive agenda than to the affective agenda. It is easier to deal with and teach facts than it is how to get along with others. Yet curricula constantly advise that the affective agenda is as important as the cognitive. Inclusion may mean for some students that the social curriculum is more important than the academic curriculum. This is determined by the most pressing needs of the individual. Fortunately, all lessons have social components and possibilities which will address the social needs of students.

As teachers we need first to recognize the social needs of our students. Secondly, we need to look at the lessons we develop for our students and consider how they might meet these social needs. It is perfectly acceptable to develop and teach lessons that address the academic needs of the majority and not to worry too much about the social part of every lesson, as long as other lessons pay attention to the social curriculum. For those students whose need is social development, however, we can put social objectives in first place and the academic objectives in second. The activity of sustained silent reading may hold the academic objective of improving reading ability for all students. It also can hold the social objective of appropriate behaviour for another student whose need is to control desire for noise or interaction at inappropriate times. The same task may serve different objectives. Sustained silent reading may be an opportunity for one student to sit near another student who needs companionship. It may be an opportunity for others to form small group to listen to a cassette tape of a book. The possibilities are without number and limited only by your flexibility and creativity.

Some spaces for your own ideas.

_____

_____

_____

_____

_____

_____

_____

_____

_____

_____

_____

_____

_____

Remember, the curriculum is controlled by the needs of our students

---
FINAL THOUGHTS

This was a quite short chapter. Some may mistake that as an indicator of relative importance. To do so would be an error of monumental size. In this instance, size is more an indication that the chapter deals with a simple truth.

Man is a social animal. Child or adult, learning is a social event before it is anything else. We do not need a lengthy and complex treatise to persuade us that we learn best in the society of others. Separating learner from learner so that they might learn better in artificially homogenous groups denies the reality of what teachers know about learning.

It may appear simple to stress a need to see the curriculum as social opportunity for learners. It also may appear simple to suggest that learning is at its strongest when diverse learners learn together. Take a look ahead at what Lev Vygotsky suggests about having learners grouped so that some can lead others on the basis of having a bit more knowledge. Truth does have a simplicity to it. Another Russian, Leo Nikolaevich Tolstoi said in the great novel *War and Peace*, "There is no greatness, where there is not simplicity, goodness, and truth.".

Be great.

VYGOTSKY AND CHILDREN'S LEARNING

You might have noticed that I bolded the name Vygotsky in the previous chapter. That is simply because his ideas are so attuned to inclusive education.

Lev Vygotsky was a Russian psychologist who developed a theory of how children learn in which Western educators have become quite interested. Vygotsky's ideas are seen to match teachers' intuitive understandings of the teaching-learning process in important ways. In particular, they may be seen to question the practice of separating children for instruction on the basis of difference in ability. Vygotsky finds considerable cognitive and affective advantage in the interactive discussion of learners at various levels of accomplishment. I like Vygotsky too. My experience is that once a teacher realizes the logic of what Vygotsky says, inclusive education becomes obvious and irresistible.

What, then, does Vygotsky say? Here are some of his basic thoughts and findings in short form.

SOCIAL BASIS FOR COGNITIVE DEVELOPMENT

According to Vygotsky learning is a social activity. It takes place most effectively in the company of others and through social interaction with these others; teachers, parents, peers, and a whole range of people who know even just a little bit more about something than does the student. Learning is not a solitary activity, but one which rests on reflective problem solving discussion with at least one partner. Limiting social interaction with more

> When students do much of their work in school by themselves, their development may be slowed. To develop fully, students must work with more skilled partners who can systematically lead them into more complex problem solving.
> McCowan, et al.

sophisticated others, such as peers, due to special education practices, may actually be detrimental to learning.

To me this is a major argument for accepting that a classroom should be organized to facilitate interaction with a range of others who can act as guides to a student. Adults are, of course, among these others. But a great resource are the other students in the class and in the school. Vygotsky suggests that peers may support and guide learning as long as they know more than does their partner. With the guidance of the teacher or other adults, peers can create a vibrant, relaxed learning environment for students with challenges to their learning.

A strategy known to most teachers is scaffolding in which new learning is approached a step at a time. Though the term was coined by the American psychologist Jerome Bruner, scaffolding is a major instructional technique which emerges from Vygotsky's thinking.

SCAFFOLDING

Scaffolding is a simple but powerful strategy known to any informed teacher. Its basis is knowing the steps to learning any new information, how the learner moves from the first tentative contact with a new area of knowledge progressively through to a reasonable objective in keeping with the student's potential. It involves the teacher selecting an appropriate learning event, defining subgoals (reminiscent of task analysis), teaching subordinate skills, and gradually reducing support as learning occurs. Scaffolding can be thought of as a series of steps.

The teacher, who is responsible for directing the overall learning of any student (target student), determines what is to be learned and the sequential steps required to reach acceptable mastery. It may be the teacher who does the actual teaching, or it may be another adult or a more advanced peer. In my view, it is best if the teacher participates in the teaching and does not hand over total responsibility to anyone else. Others may join in under the teacher's guidance to more or less degree, but the teacher has a direct teaching role, too. In keeping with fairness to all students, however, the teacher need not spend more time in direct contact with the target student than with any other student. See the later discussion under Time.

As the target student masters each step, the adult or peer guide changes the amount and/or kind of support offered. Learning becomes a continuous, interactive, reflective, problem solving discussion between learner and guide. Depending on the target student's needs and abilities the discussion may include only two individuals, or a group of learners may be involved. The key for the teacher is to determine what is to be learned, to establish the learning - teaching group, and to provide sufficient time and space for learning to occur.

MEDIATORS TO LEARNING

The content of learning is determined by the culture of the community, the family, and the school. One of Vygotsky's most significant contributions to learning theory is his stress on the cultural nature of learning. What is to be learned is what is important to the culture. The actual act of learning is facilitated by three mediators; tools for learning, language, and the behaviour of others. Mediators of learning sounds complex, but is really very straightforward. At its base is the understanding that all cultures facilitate cognitive and affective movement from one level of learning to another by using specifiable assists, and through responses to their use.

Tools for learning are the concrete or material objects you and the learner use in the act of learning. As Pick and Gippenreiter (1994) say, "This mediation may be as simple as tying a string around one's finger to help one remember something" (p. 1123). Another example would be a calculator to facilitate a math exercise. The trick is to select the right tools at the right time and to give time for enough use to cement learning.

Language is the mediator primarily employed to move beyond the concrete to the abstract. This is a process highly dependent on social interaction. Words are used to lead the learner up the steps of learning. Initially, time is taken to ensure that the learner is able to receive and understand the language necessary to new information. This time will vary from learner to learner and is a process not to be hurried. In the learning act, haste does make waste. The key is to ensure that the meaning of new language has been internalized receptively. Observation in response to language input will indicate whether new words or usages have been internalized.

The next job is to have the learner use the language to further her/his own learning.

> Children learn first to use words in social settings; they first respond to words of others, and then they use words in an interpersonal way to attract the attention or guide the behavior of others. Subsequently, they use words and language overtly to guide their own behavior.
>
> H. L. Pick & J. R. Gippenreiter

Teachers often refer to this as "Talking through a task", an "out loud" strategy employed to let an observer know what the student understands. Expression is a major step toward control of one's own behaviour and toward influencing the behaviour of others. Of course, with the students we are talking about here, oral speech may not be the expressive form. Sign, symbols, print, and other forms of expression may be employed as alternates to oral communication.

ZONE OF PROXIMAL DEVELOPMENT

All of the above lead to what is perhaps Vygotsky's most significant contribution - the concept of the Zone of Proximal Development.

The idea is that knowledge can be thought of as being divided into three fields. The first is what the student knows already. Even the most challenged student has knowledge. It may not be at the level of another student, but it is knowledge shared with other students - and known to you as well. It is just as worthwhile as any other learning and should not be denigrated simply because others have already learned it more easily or at an earlier age.

The third field is the completely unknown. We all have a lot to learn. The term "life long learning" so popular in teaching is an indicator of this reality.

Between the first and third fields is the second and most important. This is the **Zone of Proximal Development**. It is the zone where learning goes on. It can be a zone of fantastic excitement for the learner, or a zone of consistent failure. Which it is, is up to the teacher. Your pace has to be just right for any learner. Go too slowly and no advance is made in learning. Go too quickly and your student is overwhelmed.

UNKNOWN

ZONE OF PROXIMAL DEVELOPMENT

KNOWN

You are in the Zone of Proximal Development in terms of your personal learning. So am I. We all inhabit that space. Learning is available to all of us all of the time. Hopefully we will all keep advancing as we use the mediators available to us and we will learn.

In terms of your job as a teacher, your student is in the Zone of Proximal Development and needs your guidance in advancing. It is in offering this guidance that you win the accolade of being called "**Teacher**".

- What goes on in the Zone of Proximal Development is a reflection of one's culture. No matter what the level of learning or the task to be undertaken, those things mandated by your culture should be advanced.

- The dynamics occurring in the Zone of Proximal Development are social. Though the act of learning may be focused on the cognitive, it has affective components through the social interaction of guide and learner..

- Any activity within the Zone of Proximal Development is one of mediation. The mediators you have are tools of learning, language, and behaviour.

- The time spent in the Zone of Proximal Development is a function of how long it takes your learner to internalize new information. The test is one of power, not speed. Once internalization is accomplished at an acceptable level, the Zone of Proximal Development moves forward into the area of the unknown. Development has occurred, and new learning is on the horizon.

- Learning is the act of using that which is known to acquire new knowledge at the pace suitable to the learner.

- As each piece of new knowledge is mastered, the learner moves ahead and pushes the unknown back.

- Every act of learning is a move forward and to be valued as such.

This concept and the process associated with the ZPD is one of the most wonderful things for teachers. Though we may not be familiar with the fancy words, we are familiar with the fact that learning moves from the known to the unknown and then keeps repeating the cycle. It also applies to every act of learning and teaching. To me, Vygotsky has unwrapped a core pedagogical truth and made it apparent.

McCowan and colleagues (1996) have suggested the answer to the automatic question "How do I learn what the student's Zone of Proximal Development is?". They suggest that three strategies, none of which will surprise you, be used.

1. Observe your students regularly during class activities. I add to this the idea that you might talk with the parents to tap their knowledge as well.

2. Interview the student to try to find why certain answers are given or certain actions happen. Again, you might want to talk to the parents. Beyond this peers, educational assistants, and such informed others may be consulted when communication challenge is great.

3. Conduct formal assessments. I agree with the idea of assessment of learning, but I don't care for the connotations of "formal". I believe you, the teacher, can learn pretty well everything you need through the first two strategies and by routine in-class informal assessment.

THE BASICS OF VYGOTSKY

As with most profound truths, the basics of what Vygotsky says are simple.

1. Learning is a social activity which occurs between the learner and a teacher.

2. The teacher may be a professional, a parent, a peer, or any other person who knows

more than does the learner and is able to communicate that knowledge.

3. What is to be learned can be organized into a series of steps in keeping with the abilities of the learner.

4. What is needed to facilitate learning are concrete objects and materials, language, and the behaviour of interacting others.

We teachers know that what Vygotsky says is true about students and learning. We may not all know exactly who has stated these things formally, but we intuitively know the truth of the basics. What is left is to accept all learners so that our classrooms can reflect the diversity of our society, and so that all learners have maximum opportunity to learn.

STRATEGIES FOR DIFFERING ABILITY LEVELS

Students come in all sizes and shapes. They also come with all levels of abilities and needs. What you should do to support a student with challenging needs in your regular classroom depends on what the student brings to the classroom in terms of her/his abilities and needs.

The following discussion presents a view of the needs of students as falling into three broad groupings. The first group is large and includes those whose abilities are such that no sensible person would suggest that they should be placed full-time in segregated special placements. Even part-time segregation is questionable. Though many who are accustomed to the practice of withdrawing students for special one-on-one instruction, may suggest withdrawal, my experience and understanding of how children develop suggests this to be unfair to the student. It tends to come from two sources: one is an emphasis on academics without consideration of social need or effect; the other is a belief that responsibility for the student's program and progress lies with a special education teacher outside the regular classroom, rather than with the regular classroom teacher.

As you know, this manual is based on the belief that all students can benefit from regular classroom placement and that few ever benefit as much from being placed elsewhere. Certainly, those students who do not differ highly in their learning abilities should be taught in regular classrooms with regular peers. For this group of students any other plan is really questionable. The research says so and those who practice inclusively say so.

The second group is fairly large, but nowhere near the size of the first. This is a group of students with obvious challenges and whose learning occurs most strongly with modification and adaptation of content, pace, and/or instructional approach. Their needs are real and will not disappear. Teachers are not expected to work a cure. However, these students can work from much the same curriculum as others, though at a different level of demand. It is with this group that you need to demonstrate directly your teaching skills and your acceptance of the right of all students to be with their peers. You will find that you can teach members of this group well and that they will learn. But you need to understand them and to take your instruction to where they are as learners.

Students in the third group have high levels of challenge. Their needs often mean that they benefit most from individualized and/or small group curricular experiences and expectations. The social side of learning may equal or outweigh the academic. This group of students is not large at all, and the average teacher may rarely have the opportunity to teach any of its members. But when they are in your classroom, you will find that, with appropriate support, you can teach them and they will prove themselves to be learners.

The following three discussions examine the basic needs of these groups and suggest typical strategies. Room has been provided for you to keep a record of your own ideas. But first, let's look at some of the basics of modifying instruction so that we are all working from the same sheet of music.

BASICS OF MODIFYING

Regular classrooms and special education classrooms are separated by more than physical difference. They also are separated by the assumptions regular classroom teachers and special education teachers make about their teaching and their students' learning. Regular teachers tend to believe that their students can take considerable charge of their learning. The teacher's role is that of a guide, a layer out of opportunities for learning, and a guide when required. Special ed teachers tend to take charge of the student's learning and to work remedially. As Mercer, Lane, Jordan, Allsopp, and Eisele (1996) have argued, these two approaches, the implicit and the explicit, need to be blended when students with disabilities are in regular classes. Alice Udvari-Solner (1996), whose work I really admire, has provided some guidelines which may be used in the blending process and with due regard to the student's abilities and needs. The questions which follow are Udvari-Solner's. The encapsulation of her discussions under each question are mine.

- **Can the student actively participate in the lesson without modifications and achieve the same essential outcomes?**

INCLUSION: HOW TO

If so, do not burden yourself and the student with modifications. Observe, think, and decide.

- **Will student specific learning outcomes need to be identified?**

The important things to consider are what the student's educational goals in the regular class are, who is the student as a learner, and what is the quality of the student's daily participation in classroom activities. Goals will depend on educational priorities and can be modified in terms of content, application, performance expected, pace, and evaluation criteria.

- **Can the student's participation be increased by changing the instructional arrangement?**

It is known that students with disabilities fare less well in whole class and large group structures with their emphasis on student self-direction than they do in teacher directed and small group interactions in which cooperative groups and peer mediated learning are characteristic. Can you move toward the latter choice and thereby increase student involvement?

- **Can the student's participation be increased by changing the lesson format?**

This question queries use of traditional teacher driven lessons in which the teacher is possessor of important information (the curriculum) and whose role it is to transmit the information to the student (transmission model of instruction). Udvari-Solner supports a process in which all students play an active role through interactive relationships with meaningful information in a problem solving environment.

- **Can the student's participation and understanding be increased by changing the delivery of instruction or general educator's teaching style?**

The basic idea is that the teacher move toward the student's learning style and needs rather than requiring the student to try to work within the teacher's teaching style. This idea is expanded on under later discussions of Multiple Intelligences and of Learning Styles.

- **Can changes be made in the physical or social classroom environment that will facilitate participation?**

Here the physical and social environment of the classroom are considered. The society of the classroom and the culture it creates and the sheer physical realities of the classroom play roles in determining the success of inclusion. Again, you may wish to refer to the later sections looking at Learning Style, as well as the earlier one on Classroom Culture.

- **Will different instructional materials be needed to ensure participation?**

Traditionally classroom materials were developed for use by students without any particular challenges to their learning. This makes at least some of the materials inappropriate for many students with disabilities and, in fact, barriers to successful participation. Therefore, materials used with such students should take into consideration their conceptual, academic, and communication skills, and not simply be used because they work with the other students. This is not as hard as it seems. This book, for instance is sprinkled with strategies to achieve this end.

- **Will an alternative activity need to be designed for the student and a small group of peers?**

Udvari-Solner cautions that an alternate activity is not an application of the parallel curriculum in which the educational goals for a student with challenges are quite divorced form those for other students due to degree of challenge. An alternate activity is a curricular adaptation for the student and a small group of non-disabled learners which is activity based or experiential , in the same area of study as that for the rest of the class, meaningful, and age appropriate.

These questions begin at the level of students whose challenges must be understood, but which do not require substantial change to meet the same outcomes as for other students, and run through increasing degrees of change as level of challenge to learning increases. The following discussions follow a similar progression. It can be seen thinking akin to that of Udvari-Solner permeates the material. In the actual writing of the book this second set of discussions were prepared prior to inserting the Udvari-Solner questions were added to serve as a clarifying template. To me it is an indication that those who are thinking through how to arrange the regular classroom learning of students with challenges are beginning to arrive at the same spot.

LEVEL ONE

Curricular objectives in almost all areas for students with mild to moderate challenge to their learning are the same as those for the average child. You can be certain of this because the great majority of such students have degrees of challenge which do not affect academic and social functioning to any serious extent. For instance, most children who use wheelchairs will be able to do the same academic work as any other child. Children with visual challenge commonly are assisted to a great degree by properly fitted glasses or make excellent use of aids such as large print books. Of course, some adjustments to space, seating, expectations in the area of mobility, and such will be required. As a teacher you will find that you must routinely keep your student's needs in mind as you plan, but the planning will not tax you unduly. Minor modifications and adaptations will permit you and all your students to work toward the same learning and teaching objectives. When you are uncertain what to do, you can rely on a resource teacher more versed in the area of special needs, the student's parents, or other teaching colleagues to come to your assistance.

You will find that you can come up with the strategies.
The secret really is to have a positive attitude and to implement them.

AJUA encounters difficultly reading the poems and stories used in her grade five classroom. This difficulty extends to her writing as well. She can do both, but it is somewhat of a slow struggle for her. Ms Kagna has two primary methods of dealing with the reading challenge. She has set up a system in which peers quietly read incidental material to Ajua as needed in class. When time permits Ms Kagna advises Ajua's parents of upcoming reading activities and the material is read onto tapes. Sometimes volunteer students from the local high school take on this task. Similar systems have proven effective in eliciting oral responses on tests, and, of course, Ajua answers oral questions as lessons are taught. Her hearing and her speech abilities are not part of her challenge.

Through simple methods such as these students like Ajua are able to participate more routinely in classroom activities and to concentrate on their tasks. At times Ms Kagna needs to ask her resource teachers and other colleagues for suggestions, but mostly a little bit of thought and/or reference to a resource book on simple management techniques is sufficient. Once the routine of such simple modifications is familiar to class members, no additional time is usually required. The difficulties are not completely done away with, but they do not interfere as they might with the smooth conduct of the class.

OTHER STRATEGIES

A.   Use an assistant (older student, parent, volunteer) to pre-teach necessary upcoming new vocabulary, concepts, or methods.

B.   Occasionally review organization strategies such as self-monitoring, and making homework notes with the whole class. No one will be affected negatively by such strategies, and more than just the one child you might have in mind will benefit.

C.   Develop short summaries of new work with the essential material to be learned highlighted.

INCLUSION: HOW TO

D. Maintain a vocabulary list with new words and brief definitions in a location available to all for consultation.

E. Provide instructions in written as well as oral form.

F. Supplement your record of the daily schedule with simple illustrations for time and activities.

G. Arrange brief self study periods during which students can team for practice on new material. Though you may need to offer a few practice ideas, the students can be trusted to come up with new ones as they catch on to the idea of practicing with a partner.

H. Routinely use the chalkboard or an overhead to reinforce oral lessons.

I. Record activity instructions on a tape for review by students with memory needs. This can be useful for homework for many students.

J. Give practice tests to alert students to the types of questions you may ask on tests used for evaluation of progress.

K. Seat students with hearing loss away from noise sources and ensure they can see your face as you teach.

L. Have students check with buddies whether they have all the materials for the day.

M. Use portable room dividers for those who are more distractible during times when extra concentration is needed.

N.   Ask a limited number of both oral and written questions at a time.

O.   Pause after asking a question or making an important point so that all have sufficient time to process what you have said.

P.   Alter the pace of instruction for those who need a bit more time than others for writing, reading, moving.

Q.   _____

_____

R.   _____

_____

S.   _____

_____

T.   _____

_____

LEVEL TWO

While simple strategies designed to support individual needs will work for the great majority of students, there is a group of students with needs of higher order. These students may not be the most challenged, but they definitely pose a greater challenge to your teaching than does the first group of students discussed.

For this second group of students you may find that you are changing your methods more and that your curricular objectives are more fitted to individual needs and abilities. Typically, modification of lesson content, instructional outcomes, and/or evaluation methods, as suggested above, is sufficient to keep all students engaged with the same concepts and materials, though at differing levels of demand. Working in the same subject area, but at different levels of the curriculum, is sometimes referred to as the overlapping curriculum. The idea is to stay as close to the regular curriculum as possible while taking care not to exceed the abilities of some students and thereby sow the seeds of frustration and failure. This is the point where you need to exercise your teaching skills with care and use the curriculum as a guide more than as a requirement. As I write this I am reminded of the old saying, "A stitch in time saves nine." In this context I interpret it as meaning that a little advance teacher thought and preparation will save later wear and tear on both teacher and student.

LORNE experienced difficulty starting work. As soon as his grade seven teacher, Ms Staz, set a task for the class at the end of a lesson, Lorne would begin to collapse. His body would slump and his head would hang. He would whine that he did not know what to do. It certainly did not take long to note this behaviour. It occurred on the first assignment of the new school year. Immediately after a task was set, Ms Staz went to Lorne and they reviewed the task directions together. When necessary, the size of the task was modified and only one question assigned. Together they planned the steps for the task and Ms Staz wrote them down for Lorne. She then told him to go ahead with the question and went on to check on other students. As she did this she would stop by Lorne's desk occasionally to see how he was doing. When help was required she gave it. A new question was assigned as the one before was completed.

The objective was to get Lorne started and keep him working. Doing all the questions came second. Once the routine was set, Ms Staz taught it to a few of Lorne's peers and they took over. Ms Staz continued to monitor progress and to trouble shoot.

OTHER STRATEGIES

A. Restrict the number of questions associated with a task. State these clearly, write them down, and have the student repeat them.

B. For students experiencing difficulty staying on a task, try using a watch timer which will tell you it's time to check the work of a particularly distractible student. For many students a routine check will keep them on task.

C. Develop a buddy system pairing students on the basis of specific needs. A social student with one who is overly quiet; a methodical student with one who is disorganized; a reflective student with one who is impulsive. These pairings need not be only between top students and struggling students.

D. Allow a student with hard-to-read work to use a computer/typewriter.

E. Use the earlier idea of essential knowledge to reduce the amount to be learned, while still staying close to the curriculum.

F. Implement flexible deadlines for assignments and in the time set for tests. Many students can operate more strongly in flexible time situations than in speed situations.

INCLUSION: HOW TO

G.   Provide modified reading material to reduce challenge of vocabulary, syntax, and conceptual load. Volunteers can do this in school or at home.

H.   Use a cooperative learning approach.

I.   Alter the pace of instruction when necessary by teaching the same curricular area to groups of students, but at levels compatible with their abilities.

J.   _____

   _____

K.   _____

   _____

L.   _____

   _____

M.   _____

   _____

Though the students referred to at Level 2 have more significant challenge than many others, the strategies appropriate to their needs are known to most regular classroom teachers. What may be different is the degree of sophistication of the modifications and the need to contribute initial time to reap long term benefits. After the initial period of implementation and adjustment, little if any additional time is required.

It is with these students that teachers often find the need to consult with colleagues, particularly with special education resource teachers, and with parents. You are not alone in having responsibility for the student and you are not expected to know everything. As well as moving toward a collaborative approach, you may feel the need to spend more time with particular students than you believe is good for the rest of the class. If you are concerned over issues of time, see the later discussion on this topic.

LEVEL THREE

There is a comparatively small number of students whose challenges are complex and deep. In my experience this group will benefit from many of the strategies already suggested. It may take a little time to get a grasp on the complexity and depth of their needs, but you do not need to reinvent the wheel every time you meet a new student. On the other hand, you will find that you need to work with any student for a while to obtain an idea of the needs and abilities that exist. Jumping to conclusions is not recommended.

STEPHEN uses a wheelchair and has little to no verbal communication skills. Special controls are needed for his wheelchair to permit personal control of mobility. A communication system hooked up to a computer and voice synthesizer is required to support interpersonal communication. He hears perfectly well, but the synthesizer is needed to convey his wealth of thoughts and knowledge. An assistant is required to support his physical needs, but not full-time. Evaluation is by way of oral communication (speech synthesizer) and computer keyboard output. Keyboarding takes time. The electronic equipment works well with maintenance from technicians. These technicians are of value in familiarizing adults working with Stephen with the equipment. You will find that, though working with Stephen might appear daunting initially, things go more smoothly and with less challenge than you might have believed on first sight.

INCLUSION: HOW TO

Does this sound like a pipe dream? Well, I just described Stephen Hawking, the top astrophysicist in the world. Being challenged to a high degree hasn't slowed him down. What would slow him down, however, would be those who judge on the basis of appearance and then act in accordance with that judgement. Try not to prejudge your students. Have expectations **and** constantly adjust them as you gain knowledge about student strengths and needs. We are handicapped by old myths rather than current realities for many of our students.

You will find that you can figure out appropriate strategies to use with even the most challenged student. You may need support from specialist teachers, your

---
Man matures through work
Which inspires him to difficult good.
John Paul II

---

administrators, and those in other, but related, disciplines. But you will find in almost every instance that what appeared too complex at first is possible. Start at the first step and stick to basic strategies. You may need to extend your strategies, but those with which you are already familiar will work almost all the time. Have you heard of the strategy called the KISS method? This means Keep It Simple. Try the simple strategies first. Consult your parents, specialist resource teachers, and others if you find the student's needs puzzling. You may also find that the students themselves know what works for them.

This said, some students are challenged to the degree that they cannot engage the regular curriculum of your grade anywhere near that of your other students. There is no doubt in the minds of those who advocate inclusion that these student still have a rightful place in the regular classroom with their regular peers. The most normal and the most powerful environment for learning is that which we should offer all our students. Traditional educators familiar with the medical model of education may urge you to segregate some learners. If you do so, you will be choosing to limit their learning and to miss exciting opportunities as a teacher.

But what do you do when their needs are such
that the regular curriculum is not appropriate?

Many teachers move to what is called the Overlapping Curriculum. Within this approach the student works in the same curricular area as other students, but at a level suited to her/his needs and abilities. Students always work with non-disabled peers rather than being individually segregated within the regular classroom.

JOE is described as deaf-blind by his parents. In his grade four class he partakes of learning activities suited to his needs as described in his Individual Education Plan developed by his teacher, the special education support teacher, and his parents. Along with the auditory and visual challenges present, there is a suspicion that Joe has quite modest cognitive abilities. This is an uncertain area, but the blending of challenges means that Joe would experience immediate failure if expected to deal with the regular grade four curriculum.

Right now the class is working on long division using decimals. Joe is learning to match numbers of blocks with cut-out wooden numbers, along with a group of peers working on their own areas of math. In reading the class is divided into cooperative groups and writing short plays. Joe works with a group, but his reading is focused on using a magnifier to recognize pictures and words for dogs and fish, two pets at home. When the play his group is writing is preformed, Joe will be one of the case. The special ed resource teacher is in close contact with Joe's parents and all are working to begin basic math, reading, and, particularly, to stimulate social interaction at home and school.

Joe's challenges in hearing and vision make him a student most teachers will not see during their teaching careers. However, he is representative of the type of student who previously was automatically sent to a special school. The reality for most students such as Joe is that they often have usable vision and hearing, particularly with the technical aides now available. With the assistance of a good special education resource teacher for classroom support, and the support of an Educational Assistant part-time, Joe and other students like him can develop amazingly well in the regular classroom. Of course, some of the assistance he may need means he is not in the regular classroom every minute of every day. But inclusion is not meant to require unthinking adherence to the regular classroom as the only place a student may be assisted to inclusion. There are a few activities which may well be carried out outside the classroom for a period of time, but they are all designed to increase the independence of the student and to increase time with other regular students.

OLIVIA is a student in Ms Persaud's kindergarten. The room has been arranged for free passage of Olivia's electric wheelchair. Right now the class is toning up their bodies by learning to line dance. They have cleared much of the space for this activity, but space has been left for Olivia's gym mat near the windows. As her peers dance under the leadership of two students from grade eight, Ms Persaud is flexing Olivia's arms and legs in a pattern she learned from the physio. They are following the rhythms of the music to which the other students are line dancing. Olivia loves to dance.

Olivia has a symbol board on her wheelchair. She is doing well in interacting with her peers who have learned to help her hold her head up to communicate with them. She is able to ask specific children to play and talk with her now. Symbols have been created for many of the classroom activities as well as for student names. The stress on communication follows Olivia and her classmates to the playground and to the lunchroom. Symbols for her favourite foods, along with their matching words are being added to her communication list and are practiced daily, In the long run, words and letters will replace many of her symbols.

Both Olivia and Joe are good examples of higher levels of challenge being met in regular classrooms on a daily basis. The needs of such students may vary in degree, but the basic strategies are similar to those used with other children. Though working at their own levels, the Joe's and Olivia's of our world, as well as so many other children, are finding acceptance and progress in the classrooms of their neighbourhood schools in company with their neighbourhood peers.

Rather than attempt to list examples of strategies at this point, I have opted for these few general comments. The needs of the students we are talking about at this point tend to be similar to those of other students with challenges, but also to differ in degree and individuality. The good news is that once teachers decide to work with students with low to high levels of challenge, they find it quite possible. There are teachers working with children with all types of needs every day in schools not that far distant from you.

I hope that the above discussion has given you some useful ideas on how to modify and adapt for students with varying levels of need. The most valuable basic guidelines to appropriate programming which respects all students are:

- That students with differing levels of need can all attend regular classes.

- That it is of value to determine the basic level of a student and to offer curriculum at that level in the same general subject being studied by peers.

- That similar strategies work for differing levels of need.

- That teachers, parents, and others can collaborate in determining and meeting the needs of any student.

I keep returning to larger ideas such as these because focusing solely on individual strategies, modifications, and adaptations will not result in inclusion. A larger, general method of approaching a diverse community of learners is required. We do need individual ideas, but these

INCLUSION: HOW TO

must be in the context of a larger plan and a firm belief that all students are learners. It is not an impressive list of possible individual strategies that will answer our challenge, it is how we see the relationships among them and how they might be employed to achieve our larger purpose that makes us good teachers.

Well, we all need someone we can lean on,
And if you want it, you can lean on me.

Mick Jagger/Keith Richards "Let it Bleed"

Traditionally regular classroom teachers were assigned a group of students of approximately equal ability each year and expected to work on their own. The ability of the group might vary from that of other groups, but the teacher and the students were on their own, in their own room, and general strategies designed to fit the entire group developed. Inclusion and the diversity of ability of the students in a classroom means that the traditional model requires adjustment. Inclusion suggests working in teams, and cooperation, and collaboration in ways not taught in teacher preparation programs in the past. Faculties of Education are slowly catching up with what has been rapid change in the views of society about how best to deal with students with challenges. Teachers are now expected to work closely with others in planning and to welcome others into their classrooms as participants in the educational program and not just as temporary visitors. Indeed, if we can tell our students that cooperation is good for them, how can we not use cooperative/collaborative strategies ourselves?

Parents, for instance, are often uncomfortable in the school setting. This is probably due in part to natural deference to the professional educator, but also comes from distancing on the part of some teachers. A great deal is lost when teachers and parents do not communicate well. Parents have been living with the child with challenges full-time since birth. They have had to invent and try out strategies. They have had opportunity to watch what previous teachers have tried. They know, for their child, what tends to work and what doesn't better than anyone else. They can be a great asset to you in terms of planning and supporting you from the home environment. Invite them in, ask for their ideas, give them opportunities to be involved in planning. Not all will respond, but many will, and you will have strengthened your program while demonstrating the flexibility and openness needed in inclusive education.

Resource teachers are another group with whom it is valuable to consult. Many are as anxious as you are with regard to how they can help you. An inclusive approach is new to many of them. They tend to be more familiar with segregated models and withdrawal approaches than with how to support a child in a regular classroom, particularly when the degree of challenge is high. Some will work wonderfully with you from the word go. Others will be tentative, and a few domineering. Still others will press you to implement a withdrawal system in which they take some students out of your classroom for special lessons. But all will try to do what they believe best for the student. It may take some time to develop a cooperative/collaborative relationship, but the time is worth the effort.

Educational assistants are a third group with whom teachers may interact on a routine basis. These paid paraprofessionals can be a boon in a diverse classroom when worked into classroom life in appropriate ways. Some teachers are initially uncomfortable having another person consistently in the room on a full-time or part time basis. We tend not to be prepared in how to make use of an assistant. Often we feel it is inappropriate to "boss" them around. It is inappropriate to become bossy, but it is not inappropriate to take the lead in determining their role in your classroom. It is your classroom. You are the leader.

Volunteers serve many of the same purposes as do Educational Assistants. They can be a tremendous resource, particularly in situations where paid assistants are not available. Volunteers can be found in many places, if you decide that they can help you and your students.

Finally, I want to say a few words about the **principal**. This person can be a tremendous resource to you, or he/she can limit what you can achieve in including a student. In my view, teachers look to their administrators for leadership. We may complain in the staff room, but we turn to the principal when we need support and understanding. The great majority of principals will support you, if they know what you need. Often they don't as they tend to get too far away from the regular classroom in the administrator role. There are some ideas, however, which may work for you in working with your administrator to the advantage of your students and the success of your efforts.

Whatever the views of these various parties may be, you are the teacher, it is your classroom, and the student with challenges is your student as much as is any other. You may be cooperative, collaborative, and flexible, but when the child is in your class you are the ultimate decision-maker. What is decided has to work in your classroom and has to keep the child as close to the other students and the regular curriculum as possible.

So what can you do? I suggest the following generic strategies as your start line for all cooperative/collaborative relationships. It is a good idea to let people with whom you work know where you are coming from.

- Explain immediately that you believe the best place for any student is the regular classroom with regular peers.

- Stress that you welcome a collaborative relationship in which joint planning takes place and joint decisions are made.

- Focus on the belief that, whereas decisions will be made on the basis of student needs, they will be made on the basis of maintaining the child as one of the class group.

- Emphasize that any program should honour the regular curriculum to the greatest extent possible, but that you realize modifications and adaptations may be necessary.

- Communicate that strategies that take a child outside the classroom for short periods may be used, but they will be aimed at improving ability to stay in the regular classroom, and will be done in small groups rather than individually except in exceptional circumstances.

- Stress that as much as possible all students will be taught in large or small group formats, rather than one-on-one. The latter serves to segregate the child within the classroom.

■   Be firm that you will teach all your students, regular and included personally, as well as setting up opportunities for others to work with them. All students belong to all who work in the classroom.

Cooperation/collaboration is a major support for inclusion. As teaching becomes more complex and the teacher is faced with reforms such as inclusion, the way we teach, the way we understand our roles as teachers, and whom we regard as students must change. Change is a necessary element in education. Education, with its central importance to the future, cannot afford to cling too firmly to the past.

The following discussions expand on how the teacher and each of the above groups might work together to the advantage of all students.

INCLUSION: HOW TO

> ## *PARENTS*

Education systems have held parents at a distance. Traditionally, we have preferred to advise them periodically through report cards of how well their children were doing, only asking them to visit the school if a problem arose. The parent-teacher association, which included only a few parents and teachers, was the sole point of routine contact in most schools. Recently school councils have developed as parents and parent advocates lobbied for increased involvement. Even these bodies involve few parents and too many in the education system do their best to downplay the idea. Most teachers view parents sort of as interlopers in the school, people who visit for meet the teacher night and the annual play, but who are not an integral part of what happens at school.

Thinking is beginning to create change though. Parent councils with parents playing a role in running schools are one evidence of this. Another is the collaboration between some teachers and parents in support of students with disabilities. Teachers are finding that parents have experience and knowledge about their children; experience and knowledge of value in planning and implementing an Individual Education Plan (IEP). Parents are discovering that teachers really care about students and are willing to collaborate to strengthen a program.

There is a great deal to be gained from parents and teachers communicating and collaborating. This is true for all students, but particularly so for students with high levels of need. Most teachers have not worked with such students and wonder what to do, how to begin, and how will things go. The parents have been there. They have worked with their son or daughter for years and have learned a great deal which can benefit the teacher. If you are willing to be open and to value the contributions parents can make, you will find your job easier. The parents will understand what you are going through and they will appreciate your acceptance of their child and your efforts. The collaboration of teacher and parent is another proof that:

> ## TOGETHER WE ARE BETTER

What does working with parents mean? First let me say what it does not mean for me. It does not mean that the parent runs your program. It does not mean that you must do whatever the parent says. It does not mean that the parent is in the school and classroom every day.

What teacher-parent collaboration does mean is that:

- You and the parents are in routine communication to the extent that communication is necessary and comfortable.

- Parents are invited to contribute to the program planning and trouble shooting.

- Parents are kept advised of achievements and sticky points in the program.

- You and the parents discuss how the parents can support your program at home and how you can support their program at school.

- The parents support you and you support them in keeping the program on track.

- Parents are involved in important decisions in their child's program.

You will rarely run into trouble with parents, if you show that you respect them and their knowledge and want to include them in the school program in reasonable ways.

> ### *Suggested Strategies*

- Call the parents and invite them in when their child is included in your class.

- Ask them what they hope for their child that year.

INCLUSION: HOW TO

- Ask them how they would like to see their involvement in their child's program work out over the year.

- Tell them you would value their input in developing the IEP. If you do this, think about the timing of meetings.

- Set up a routine communication plan with the parents.

- Think about a communication book, an e mail link, or a weekly phone call.

- Ask the parents to keep you informed of things which happen at home which may have meaning in the school context.

This may sound like a lot, but much of it will fall into a routine which takes little time after it is set up. Most parents will not wish routine involvement in the school program, and will be content to trust you to do your best. For parents who wish to be involved, see it as a way to strengthen the program and forestall misunderstandings. Their attendance at routine meetings will not take more of your time. Involving the parent simply places a particularly knowledgeable person at the planning table. For instance, the parent brings experience with their child's learning style and has found ways to call on aspects of intelligence sometimes not thought of by teachers. The gain in support and understanding is well worth the extra effort you may put forth.

RESOURCE TEACHERS

A knowledgeable and flexible resource teacher (RT) can be a boon to your inclusion program. First of all the RT is a teacher, and very often a teacher with extensive knowledge of special needs, teaching strategies, how to locate materials and supplies, how to work with parents and others, and reporting methods. Frequently the RT also has experience supporting students with special needs and their teachers in the regular classroom environment.

A word of caution, however. I have known RT's whose background and professional conviction lead them to believe that segregating some students in special classes or on a withdrawal basis is to be preferred. They will support you with your students, but may suggest dependency on out-of-classroom programming when progress is slow or when behavior is a challenge. Even when in your classroom, they may prefer one on one teaching. It is difficult to leave old strategies behind when difficulties arise.

As mentioned previously, some out-of-classroom activities may be called for on a limited basis, if they will address certain needs which cannot be met in the classroom. Let your RT know that for you being inclusive does not mean rigid adherence to being in the regular classroom come hell or high water. It does mean that out-of-class activities must be weighed for their contribution to the inclusion experience. I suggest that you make your view of how the program in your classroom should run quite clear to the resource teacher right away. The suggestions made in the introduction to this section on Cooperation and Collaboration may help you here.

Fortunately, most resource teachers will work with you to develop the program which you feel would work best in your classroom. And they are teachers, so they have a grasp of curriculum and overall classroom management that others will not bring to the development and implementation of your program. They can be your most important program support.

INCLUSION: HOW TO

You may find these suggestions helpful.

Working with the Resource Teacher

- Be proactive. Approach the RT and ask for her/his support before he/she approaches you.

Most RT's will appreciate you asking for assistance, and you will have demonstrated that every student, including those with special needs, is your responsibility.

- Try to handle things yourself before you request assistance from an RT.

It is my experience that resource teachers often enter the picture too soon and begin to establish themselves as the person who knows most about your student's special needs. RT's are wonderful people, but you do not need to set up any dynamic which suggests that there is a difference in how you regard students with challenging needs, and your responsibility to them. Establish your role as teacher of the entire class first and at the same time learn something about the child's needs and abilities yourself.

- Involve the RT as a core member of the IEP planning team as soon as you have an idea of what support your student appears to need.

When my daughter-in-law Patricia first began to teach students with challenging needs, their IEP's were already written and she was expected to follow them without question. Her input to planning how she and her students would begin the year was not invited. I find that the IEP often is written before the teacher meets the child. I cannot think of a better way to ensure that you feel you don't really have responsibility for the child. An IEP is necessary in many cases, but it should not be developed before you know what the child's needs and abilities are. The IEP should reflect your knowledge of the child, your approach to teaching, and your approach to inclusion. Of course, it will reflect the RT's views, the parents' views, and perhaps the views of others. But you are the child's future for this year. You must have a major role in such basic decisions.

- Think about the role you would like to see the RT play in support of your program. In an inclusive program the RT supports the teacher and the special needs students in a classroom, not by withdrawing the child. There are a number of possibilities for how this support is realized.

I have seen RT's serve as a co-teacher in a classroom for whatever parts of the day he/she is there. The two teachers plan part of the regular program together and one teaches the class while the other assists students individually or in small groups. Roles are exchanged. When it is necessary to work one -on -one with any student, either teacher may do this.

Some teachers prefer the RT to work with individuals or small groups to develop or bolster certain skills. In this model the focus of the RT is on students with special needs. The drawback to it is that the regular teacher assumes a secondary role with these students.

RT's may serve as facilitators. In this role, the RT sets up meetings, suggests teaching strategies, locates supplies and materials, communicates with parents and other support personnel, writes reports, and assists with program planning. He/she ensures that things run smoothly.

Of all of these, the one I prefer is the first. I like to have a role in teaching the full class, small groups, and individuals. It gives me a chance to interact with all the students and to model my approach for all students. It also gives me a first hand knowledge of how each student is learning and feeling in my classroom.

- Discuss and plan the role you and the RT will assume with the RT.

Even though I recommend that you think through the RT role in advance, I do not suggest that you come to a firm decision on the role until you and the RT meet. Both of you will have ideas of how to work together. I do recommend that you have some basic positions, such as that every students will be a part of the class and rarely singled out if it can be avoided. But don't pre-decide everything. However, well intentioned people can come to agreement on how they will work together to the advantage of students.

- Be flexible.

All the things you plan initially may need to change as progress is made or not made, as opportunities arise, and as other supports are made available or disappear. Keep the communication channel open between you and the RT. Together, you can work wonders with students that others would consider not worth the effort.

EDUCATIONAL ASSISTANTS

An Educational Assistant (EA) is that extra pair of hands teachers sometimes need to deal effectively with a large and diverse classroom group, or to provide the level of support required to include students with high level challenges. EA's often are hired with little knowledge of disability and even less of teaching. Their backgrounds may include some preparation in an EA program, but this is usually not the case. However, they have a great deal to contribute to the welfare and progress of your students, if you provide the guidance and leadership they need.

As noted previously, most teachers have had no preparation for working with EA's. Most principals also have no experience with EA's other than of a general nature. They may have hired some in response to particular situations, but will have no particular depth of understanding of how they are to be guided and employed. The majority of principals will have some understanding of integration, but not of inclusion. This is in keeping with their background and the principal's role, which tends to be administrative rather than practice oriented. A good resource teacher may be able to give you some ideas, but most also have little experience with an EA in a regular classroom environment. In addition to this, most EA's with experience will have gained that in special classes or under the integration model.

This is not a criticism of principals, of resource teachers, or of educational assistants. It is simply the reality that inclusion is a new reform which has come on so rapidly that many educators have little background in it. Unless their school system adopts inclusion as a policy, they are expected to maintain the older model of segregating some students and integrating others. As noted at an earlier point, there is a real difference between inclusion and integration. Integration agrees that some students should be fully segregated while others are permitted in the regular classroom on a part time to full time basis. Inclusion does not agree with placing any student outside of the regular classroom on a regular, long term basis

This means you are on your own in most instances as you proceed with your plan to teach inclusively. Others will offer you general support, but inclusion is most likely new to them too. Luckily, there are some basic guidelines which will help you work with the EA in the interest of inclusion. Some were already given under the introduction to this section on Cooperation and Collaboration. They suggest that you let the EA know your intent to run an inclusive classroom and to share responsibility for all students. Those that follow are more pragmatic.

- Request that you are permitted to meet with prospective EA's to get an idea of how they think and whether you will be able to work together. If you don't do this, your principal or some other system level person will simply assign an EA sight unseen.

- Ask if your system has an EA job description. If so, get a copy so you know what the EA expects the job to be. This is of particular importance if the EA belongs to a union and there is a negotiated job description.

- If there is no job description, write down the types of things you would like the EA to do in your classroom. Your resource teacher may be a real help in this planning. Keep your points fairly general, but student oriented. Run your ideas past the principal and explain what you are trying to do.

- Expect the EA to work with any student, even though focusing on one or two specific students. You don't want to limit the flexibility of the classroom. Too specific and close an EA - student relationship can foster dependency.

- Avoid at all costs giving the EA or anyone else the idea that the EA is assigned to one student. This point is so important, I'm repeating it.

- Set up a flexible routine of daily responsibilities which may change with time.

- Be prepared to direct the EA's overall interactions with any student or group of students in terms of deciding what is to be taught, practiced, or reviewed.

Once the EA is assigned, discuss your job expectations and be prepared to accept some EA suggestions. Stress that flexibility is an aim and some things may change with time and experience.

- Make certain that you plan for EA breaks and that they occur at routine times.

- Spend a few minutes at the beginning of each day discussing the day's activities.

- Spend a few minutes at the close of each day reviewing the day's events and planning for the next day.

- As the student progresses, experiment with reducing EA support. A crutch is not needed forever, for the student or for you.

I do not care to think in negatives, but there is one suggestion I have for what not to do with an EA.

- Do not treat your EA as a person to do odd jobs such as putting up bulletin boards, photocopying, or preparing your lunch.

Some teachers actually do these things and waste the EA as a support to students. Of course, you do need to do some routine chores. I suggest that your and your EA share them.

The verse which follows also may give you some ideas of how to work with EA's.

Remember at all times that you are the teacher, all the students in your room are your responsibility before anyone else's. Though you may be cooperative and collaborative with others in your classroom, you are the prime decision-maker in the interests of the students.

The Educational Assistant's Prayer

I wish for a teacher who will see me as

a colleague with contributions to make.

I wish for a teacher who will see me as an assistant

to all children,

though with particular focus on a few.

I wish for a teacher who will ask for my ideas.

I wish for a teacher who will see me as a person,

but feel free to guide me as a tool

to benefit children.

I wish for a teacher who will challenge me

to do my best.

I wish for a teacher who likes children.

I wish for a teacher in whom I can see a model.

Gary Bunch

VOLUNTEERS

Paid Educational Assistants will not always be available to assist you in your classroom. In fact, often a paid EA is not the answer to your needs. There are many situations in which you could use an extra pair of hands for a specific time each week, or for a day or two. It is not simply a matter of saying "I have been assigned children with special needs. Therefore, I need an Educational Assistant or I cannot manage". I always suggest that you try working with the students by yourself first and that you use the information gained during this time to determine if you really do need an extra pair of hands, and, if so, how much help you need, when, and why. Every decision you take in your classroom should be aimed at a proven need. Teachers are professionals, not only because they have a certificate saying so, but also because they know about children and learning, teaching, and classroom management.

So, where will you find an extra pair of hands? The answer is "At the end of the arms of volunteers of all ages, genders, and backgrounds". I have seen many creative teachers decide to try volunteers and, as long as they were prepared to do a little spade work, they found what they were looking for. In fact, if you have a good Resource Teacher or a proactive principal, you may find that they view finding people to assist you to be part of their responsibility. In the case of the Resource Teacher, work it out in your early discussions about roles in support of students with special needs. Often the Resource Teacher's timetable is flexible enough to permit her/him to take on this role. In other instances, your principal may have delegated someone on staff to coordinate volunteers.

Here are examples of some of the volunteers I have seen assisting in regular classrooms.

■   **Students in the school.**

Every school has a wealth of capable, enthusiastic volunteers just waiting to be asked. That is one of the magnificent things about children. They love to help. They love to do something different. They love to feel needed. You are familiar with peers helping peers of the same age and older students reading and tutoring younger ones. This can work for you. And don't think that just because a student has some challenging need, he or she cannot be a super peer helper. As long as the student has the knowledge and the time, the student can be a helper. It can be a positive experience for them as well.

■ **Parents.**

You have as many parents connected to the school as you have students. Obviously, most of them will not be in a position to volunteer in your classroom due to other commitments. But some will be able to. Ask your principal to send a note home asking if any parent would like to help out on a regular basis with a student at school. Outline the type of help and give the school phone number. The secretary can pass the numbers to you and you can call. This works almost every time.

Three cautions if you pick up on this idea.

1. I do not suggest using parents from your own classroom and, particularly, the parents of the child you wish to support. This can work out, but, as you can imagine, there could be tricky aspects to it. Your parents can volunteer for other teachers and vice versa.

2. Do not send volunteer requests home with too many students. You may end up with more than you can use. Check with one of your colleagues and ask if the request notes can be sent out to her/his parents. If no volunteer comes forth, try another class.

3. Know what you want your volunteer to do. I find that it is necessary in most situations to stress that the volunteer must be available at a regular time or times. You need to be able to plan the volunteer into your program.

■ **Community members.**

All communities have people who would like to offer some time to a good cause. They just don't know how to make contact, or they would need to travel too far, or the time required doesn't fit their schedules. All of these problems can be taken care of. Local synagogues, churches, mosques, and their equivalents often will make an announcement for you at their services or post a note on their bulletin boards. Other community organizations will do the same. As for travel, most community schools are within walking distance of the entire community. Your ability to make use of an hour here and there to support a student permits volunteers to devote a minimum of time going to and from the school.

■ **Secondary school students.**

Every community elementary school has a secondary school which its students attend. This secondary school is filled with bright, enthusiastic, older students, some of whom would love to gain experience with your class. A perfect set up is a secondary school with a cooperative education or a family life program. Teachers running such programs are looking for placements for their students. It could be a perfect marriage. Beyond that, secondary students may be interested in volunteering during their spares, or as part of a course. The flexibility of timetables at the secondary level, and the creativity of many secondary school principals and teachers make these schools a good bet.

■ **Community colleges and universities.**

What was just said for secondary schools, goes for community colleges and universities. There are programs at these centers directed to the study of children, schools, and students with special needs. And all of them need sites for practicing what they are learning.

■ **Senior citizen's centers.**

Some people tell me that I'm way off on this one, but they are wrong. Intergenerational

INCLUSION: HOW TO

relationships can work wonders. The older folks in our community have a great deal to offer. Most are still active, interested, and willing to give. Some may be at a local activity center and others may be residents in a senior citizen home. Among them will be found mothers, fathers, uncles, and aunts with a world of experience with children. They will also have a variety of backgrounds, including many with knowledge in the areas you are teaching. They may need a ride to and from your school, but you will find that there are community clubs who can offer rides if they know the exact times.

I have even seen a program that used volunteers from a local prison. While this may strike some as overly creative, it worked well. The volunteers wanted something to do. They had the time. The prison saw it as rehabilitation and had the transport. Think and act creatively. Don't limit your options.

Though volunteers are not paid to work with you, the same suggestions as made for working with Educational Assistants apply. They, and you, will benefit from having a clear idea of what is expected of them and how you will support them in your work, and they you. They will be giving your students something, but the children will be giving them something right back.

If you need that extra pair of hands, don't weep and gnash your teeth. Do something about it. You will find that your efforts will be rewarded. Perhaps not right away, but give it time and you will find volunteers on whom you can rely.

PRINCIPALS

Take, as a beginning point, that the average principal is the most important support you can have as a teacher. Then take as a second point, that the average principal has experience with integration, but none with inclusion. Integration has been around for some time and inclusion is just becoming known. Your principal will be working from an integration viewpoint, and that viewpoint accepts that routinely sending some students out of the regular class for special instruction is how schools should operate. They believe it is good for the students, good for the regular class, and good for the regular class teacher. Inclusion says that this is not the strongest educational model, but the average principal believes it to be the case. He/she may not understand how a student with disabilities can do better in your class than with a special teacher in a more protected environment at least part of the time.

You are interested in inclusion and know that you can run a classroom in which all students will benefit and no one will lose anything. Your job, then, is to let your principal know that you can include students, that they will achieve both academically and socially at least as well as they would in a segregated environment, that the education of the other students will not suffer, and that you will last out the year.

Fortunately, you have the experiences of other inclusive teachers, a mounting pile of supportive research, and your own abilities and philosophy on your side. Fortunately, as well, almost every principal wants children to be together if at all possible, and to do well.

HOW CAN YOU CONVINCE YOUR PRINCIPAL?

- Sit down and talk to her/him about what you want to do in your classroom and why.

- Point to government policy supporting placement in the regular class as the placement of first choice for every child. (More and more federal, state, and provincial governments are announcing such policies.)

- If your government does not yet have such a policy, point to those educators who are teaching inclusively and successfully. Emphasize the "leading edge" nature of inclusion and the general movement of education to inclusion.

- Lay out your plan for beginning and your plans to collaborate with parents, resource teachers, and others.

- Offer some of the research documenting the positive nature of inclusion for all students, the desire of people with disabilities to be included in community, and the desire of many parents to have their children educated with their peers.

I lay quite a bit of stress on letting your principal know your plans because I believe the principal is a key. If the principal supports you, other colleagues, including resource teachers, regular class teachers, and educational assistants will too. In addition, you can anticipate support in obtaining materials and equipment, planning time, outside specialist support, and whatever else appears reasonable, or close to it.

Part of why I stress the principal's role, also, is that I have been a classroom teacher and a principal. I know how I thought about principals when I was in the classroom. I know how isolated a principal can feel if teachers do not communicate. I know that both of you want the best for students. Again, together we can be better. Ignore the staff room complainer and keep going.

The next step is to work with your principal as you implement your inclusive program. Above all, don't keep your principal in the dark. An informed principal is often a supportive, interested principal.

Many teachers, when first thinking about including students with challenging needs in their classrooms, think about the time inclusion may take. The amount of time you have in a day and the number of students you have in your class must be balanced so that, over time, all receive a fair share of your attention. Time management is a priority for all teachers, whether or not students with challenging needs are included in their classes. Many teachers have told me that inclusion takes some more time, particularly at the beginning. They also have told me that the time is worth the reward for them and their students.

In my experience the major questions regarding time are:

1. How can I address the needs of this particular student and yet be fair to all the others?

2. How will I find time for planning and to meet with other professionals and parents to keep the program moving?

Such questions are of valid concern and must be taken seriously. You need to think them through and plan strategies to cope with the issue of time. Fortunately, the thoughts and experiences of others will come to your aid.

How will I address the needs of this particular student and yet be fair to all the others?

My answer to this is that: (a) you must be ruthless and (b) you must have a clear idea of what the student's needs and abilities are. These two are closely intertwined.

Teachers are people who respond to their students. When they see a child struggling to learn, they leap to the child's assistance. When need is great, they believe response must be great.

Many feel they must assist the student to do better than ever before, and to match the class academically and socially. Very often this translates into pressure to support the student intensively and extensively - to spend a lot more time with her/him than with other students.

TO DO SO IS A MISTAKE!

The feeling that a student's needs are great and that you must respond to them is not the mistake. Deciding to spend more time with that one student than with others on a routine basis is. As a teacher, out of the need to be fair to all the others, you must make the apparently ruthless decision not to give the student extra time. But is this fair to the student who is included?

Yes, it is. If you have thought things through and have developed some strategies to deal with the situation.

First of all, accept that you cannot disproportionately distribute your time. That would be unfair to the other students and frustrating to all. This is your basic starting position.

Secondly, think of what you know about learning. You know that you cannot cure a student of a challenging condition. Child development does not work like that and you are not a doctor. You can assist a student's learning, but you cannot cure the problem in most cases.

If you do give that student more time at the expense of other students, will it have been worth it in terms of actual learning? This is really doubtful. We all learn within our capacity to learn and at our own pace. Students with challenging needs are students whom we know do not learn for one reason or another, with the same ease as do other students. Why, then, do we believe we should require them to benefit from more direct teaching than any other student with the idea that they will learn faster than ever before? Your teaching must be paced to the student's ability to take in new information, retain it, and demonstrate that learning has taken place. You cannot make students learn more than they can take in. Have a look at the earlier discussion of Vygotsky and the Zone of Proximal Development. Movement from the known to the unknown is gradual and individually determined. Better to decide how much time you have to spread over all your students and do so evenly. Of course, from day to day time will not be even, but over time it should be. This may appear a ruthless suggestion, but it is also fair and will result in maximum progress for all involved.

If you have a student who needs more stimulation than you have time for personally, your strategy should be getting another pair of hands, an educational assistant, a resource teacher, a volunteer, a peer tutor, on a regular basis. I am not saying that you hand over responsibility for planning for and teaching the student. These are your responsibilities, though they may be shared with others. What I am saying is that you must make logical decisions and then act on them.

Think things through. Use your knowledge of human development.

Be ruthless in being fair to all.

> ## How will I find the time for planning to meet with other professionals and parents in order to keep the program moving?

For many students with challenging needs an IEP is mandated by legislation and/or local practice. This means spending a certain amount of initial time and then monitoring and updating the IEP as time goes on. The collaborative nature of IEP planning in inclusion means that the planning is done while you are at school. Where does the time come from during the school day without eating up the time you need for yourself and other responsibilities?

My experience is that the problem of time is related to the way schools organize teacher time. Only certain times, before class in the morning, at lunchtime, and after school, traditionally are viewed as planning time with colleagues, parents, and others. More recently some schools have begun to set up group planning time for teachers at the same grade level during the day, but not as planning time for individual students. Yet time must be found. If it is not, the teacher will become frustrated at having to use personal time, collaboration will not be possible, and the result will be planning which is not as good as it could and should be.

Creative trade-offs can provide an acceptable solution. I use the term "creative" because I think we need to find ways to plan during the school day, and not only at the three traditional times. Though only a few teachers may need extra daytime planning due to the distribution of students with challenges, everyone in the school must become creative in addressing what is, after all, a problem for the whole school. You have the child this year. Another will have her next year, and another the year after. It takes a whole school to teach a child.

I have seen the following ideas used to good effect.

- Rather than you leading IEP development and monitoring, the resource teacher could, with you in a collaborative role. RT's often have flexible timetables, they have knowledge of challenging conditions, and they are there to support you.

- Collaborate with a teaching colleague in taking care of two classes for a specific period of time, thus freeing up time for both of you on a regular basis.

- Collaborate with the principal or vice principal to have them take responsibility for your class during short, regularly scheduled times. Believe it or not, they are teachers and they need to keep in touch with practice.

- Collaborate with your principal and the staff to arrange for a supply teacher once a month or so to take a series of classes on regularly scheduled planning days.

- Make use of time available when your class takes some other subject with another teacher (e.g. phys. ed., art, etc.).

These types of ideas may not solve every time problem, but they will lessen the problem. I have found that most teachers and principals are willing to collaborate in creative fashion, if needs are explained. They really do want to support you, but sometimes they need to be kickstarted just like a car. Once they are running, good things can happen.

A central tenet of inclusive education is that difference is a reason to be in the regular classroom, not a reason to be excluded from it. Supporting this position are beliefs such as "Children learn better together, than when separated by level of ability", and "The classroom should reflect the local community in its diversity".

Traditional views of difference in ability are that students should be separated if tests and/or achievement suggest that the difference is large. Often a two year difference is used as the marker. The most meaningful instrument to those who hold the test-oriented view, is the test of intelligence or IQ. Many problems have been found with IQ tests, most of which commonly are viewed as biased against difference in race and culture. They are also considered biased against ability due to their narrow focus on reading, mathematical, memory skills, and average behaviour. Theories of intelligence which lead to such narrowly defined tests are restrictive and artificial. Robert Sternberg, editor of the *Encyclopedia of Human Intelligence*, points to the narrowness of such tests when he says, "None of the conventional intelligence tests or achievement tests measure creative abilities" (1989, p. 6). This is only one weakness of traditional, standardized tests.

Recently Howard Gardner (1983) has challenged traditional views of intelligence with the theory of multiple intelligences. Though so new and taking such a different approach that it is still considered controversial and unproven by many traditional theorists, it has been embraced by a host of educators and has led to change in teaching practice in a wide range of classrooms. Its attractiveness lies in the fact that Gardner rejects the idea that intelligence is restricted to a limited set of abilities. He also rejects tests of intelligence and suggests developing portfolio assessment over time as a stronger way to observe the changing abilities of students.

Gardner suggests a wide range of abilities which are culturally determined and, therefore, which may change as culture changes. Initially, Gardner laid out seven intelligences, but recently and eighth, an intelligence having to do with understanding of the natural world, has been added (Checkley, 1997). Kathleen Whitbread (1996), editor of *The Inclusion Notebook*, cites Thomas Armstrong's definitions of the first seven, and I have added the most recent.

- **LINGUISTIC:**   Intelligence of words.
- **LOGICAL/MATHEMATICAL:**   Intelligence of reasoning and numbers.
- **SPATIAL:**   Intelligence of images and pictures.
- **MUSICAL:**   Intelligence of tone, rhythm, and timbre.
- **BODILY/KINESTHETIC:**   Intelligence of body and hands.
- **INTRAPERSONAL**   Intelligence of self-knowledge.
- **INTERPERSONAL:**   Intelligence of social understanding.
- **NATURALIST:**   Intelligence of the natural world.

The view of an array of interlocking intelligences maintains attention to academically related abilities such as language and math, and opens up many other areas in which any student can show capability. As has been said about multiple intelligences:

> **THE QUESTION NO LONGER IS "HOW SMART IS THE STUDENT?", BUT HOW IS THE STUDENT SMART?".**

In the classroom of a teacher who accepts multiple intelligences as a working concept, a student who differs in ability no longer needs to be judged solely in terms of verbal, linguistic, and mathematical achievement. As Armstrong (1944) notes, we all have capacity in each area of intelligence. The degree of challenge experienced by some students in their learning may mean that they will achieve more modestly than others, but all can be guided to higher levels, if all their strengths are recognized. With multiple intelligences thinking the teacher has many valid areas through which to plan for and to assess progress. And students have many more ways in which they can exhibit developing ability. Who could ask for more?

Some Examples

Nicky is stronger in drawing than in reading and writing, subjects in which she struggles to stay with her class. Ms Ryan, her language teacher, while the other students are writing answers to questions, often has a story read to Nicky and encourages her to draw pictures of what happens in the story as a way of showing her knowledge.

Miro's primary contribution to a group project is directing the arrangement of the group's final products of print, illustrations, and graphs on a display board. Though his motor skills are not up to speaking, printing, and drawing, he has an eye for design.

Encouraging and applauding the efforts of others is **Sharif's** forte. Though challenged in his physical abilities, he can tell when one of his friends needs a "You can do it." smile and a pat on the back. His confidence in their abilities motivates the other students.

Angela takes on the job of reading the history material to her partner Cindy. Cindy's memory for words is fine, but she cannot maintain her concentration when reading by herself.

Marika can really relate to people. Both **Mark** and **Riva** feel comfortable when it is Marika's turn to monitor their work. They can understand her explanations of mathematics because she makes the problems seem straightforward to them. They can do the computations once they have been guided through the steps.

Jon is not too good at stuffing the basketball. He can't get the height from his wheelchair. But he is a talented dribbler and can keep the ball away from anyone as he moves up the floor to make a pass.

Maria's work for the assignment on weaving necklaces is to keep everyone supplied with the right colours of gimp. Without her the project of making necklaces for fund raising would move along much more slowly. She has a way of helping unobtrusively but in a friendly way.

While the rest of the class is working on paper and pencil adding and multiplying problems, **Judy** keeps pace using her abacus. She finds that her wand really helps in moving the beads about. She enjoys her math and does well in it.

When the class decided to sing "The Little Drummer Boy" for the school concert, **Norm's** speech challenge wasn't a factor. His drumming talents fit in well on the big night.

The idea of intelligence as a developing instead of as a static ability is intuitively accepted by teachers who believe they can guide students to improve. No longer need students be held to a lockstep curriculum in which they are held back in some areas until others catch up when curriculum is viewed as flexible. Multiple intelligences encourages teachers to push ahead flexibly and to take advantage of all capacities in reaching toward the future.

> **The purpose of school should be to develop and use the intelligences**
> **to help a person reach vocational and avocational goals**
> **appropriate to her/his particular spectrum of skills.**
>
> (Gardner, 1987, p. 190)

Education is use of the period during which the young child or the youth is most rapidly developing to prepare for the most positive possible future. Strategies such as multiple intelligences support this preparation more powerfully for all students regardless of any type of difference. This is the type of strategy which supports inclusion.

PORTFOLIOS AND AUTHENTIC ASSESSMENT

The particular gift of multiple intelligences is its positive nature. Proponents are no longer concerned with traditional tests, but have moved to portfolio assessment wherein development over time can be seen through observation of the student and the student's work. The traditional curriculum does not control all learning which is now based on student needs and abilities. All students are seen as learners in their own rights, not divided into achievers and non-achievers.

Many students with challenging needs do not fare well under traditional testing. As noted, IQ tests are limiting for many with challenges. In addition, standardized testing assumes that what the student has learned is quantifiable, that the student can work at her/his best level without the support of teachers or peers, and that the passive student role in assessment permits full involvement in the process (Gelb-Shuhendler, 1998). Such assumptions are false for any student, and more so for students with challenging needs. As Earl and Cousins (1996) argue, a method of assessment leading to adjustments in learning is to be preferred and traditional testing fails at doing this. The development of portfolios gives the student a better chance to show strengths and needs, and provides the teacher a clearer view of those strengths and needs.

Armstrong (1994, pp. 128-129) summarizes the uses of portfolios as:

- **Celebration:** To acknowledge and validate students' products and accomplishments during the year.
- **Cognition:** To help students reflect on their own work.
- **Communication:** To let parents, administrators, and other teachers know about the student's learning progress.
- **Cooperation:** To provide a means for groups of students to collectively produce and evaluate their own work.
- **Competency:** To establish criteria by which a student's work can be compared to that of other students or to a standard or benchmark.

You know enough about inclusion now to realize that all of these agree with inclusive philosophy. Authentic assessment, as exampled in portfolios, honours individual learning, provides a clear view of individual progress, and gives the student and teacher information which will help build an educational program.

As the year goes by and you and your students develop portfolios, you will find that they contain:

- Photographs of events, actions, and projects.
- Interview notes from discussions with peers, parents, and others.
- Notes recording anecdotes or personal accomplishments and effort.
- Videotapes of work habits, socialization, and projects.
- Checklists of skills and behaviours.
- Student writings.
- Cassette tapes of speeches, reading, and linguistic development.
- Art samples showing use of different techniques and media.
- Exercises in various subject areas.
- Informal test results.
- Student charts, graphs, and maps.
- Anything else you and your students believe indicates how the student is doing.

These and other evidences of learning over time are welcome evidence of learning. They can also spark ideas for all students to communicate progress and needs to others.

You will notice that the various ideas presented under multiple intelligences do not call for any basic change in your teaching or assessing of progress. Most teachers do things such as those suggested as a part of their ordinary teaching. In my experience the difference is that you have a background guide about student learning in multiple intelligences which frees you up to see students as individuals all of whom are learners, and all of whom you can teach, particularly in collaboration with colleagues and parents. Any change required is more one of attitude than practice.

The move to realizing the benefits of multiple intelligences
does not require manifold change in your teaching.
It does require widening your view of what intelligence is
and then directing instruction to needs and abilities.

INCLUSION: HOW TO

Beyond adopting multiple intelligences as part of the way you approach running the classroom, what is needed is simply good, child oriented teaching, teaching to which all teachers aspire. The following charts developing aspects related to each of the intelligences reinforce the fact that using multiple intelligences theory is no more than intuitively good teaching. A broad concept of what constitutes intelligent activity such as that contained in multiple intelligences, coupled with the skills of a flexible, thoughtful teacher promises much in terms of all students reaching their individual potentials.

GARDNER'S EIGHT INTELLIGENCES & TEACHING IDEAS

INTELLIGENCE	ATTRIBUTES	STUDENT ENJOYS	STRATEGIES
LINGUISTIC -USE OF WORDS	USING LANGUAGE IN VARIOUS FORMS	-CHATTING -VERBAL ACTIVITIES -READING -WRITING -WORD GAMES -NEW WORDS -WORD SOUNDS	-VERBAL/WRITING ACTIVITIES -GROUP PROJECTS -PRESENTATIONS -DICTIONARY WORK -DEBATING - WORD GAMES -DRAMA/ROLES
LOGICAL/MATH -REASONING & RULES	USING LOGICAL APPROACHES TO PROBLEM SOLVING	-CLASSIFYING -ESTIMATING -LISTS, NOTES -ASKING QUESTIONS -MATH/GEOMETRY -PATTERNS	-COMPUTATION -DIAGRAMS/GRAPHS -NUMBER PROBLEMS -MAPS & PICTURES - LOGIC & STRATEGY -SCIENCE FAIRS -DEMONSTRATIONS
VISUAL - SPATIAL -IMAGES & PICTURES	DAY DREAMING PICTURING EVENTS ARRANGING & EXAMINING RELATIONSHIPS OF OBJECTS	-PLAYING WITH SHAPES -ART & DRAWING -DECORATING -GAMES WITH MOVEMENT -ASSEMBLING & DISASSEMBLING	-FIGURE-GROUND ACTIVITIES -ART & DRAWING -MAPPING -ROLE PLAY -BUILDING THINGS -MOVEMENT IN SPACE GAMES

INCLUSION: HOW TO

INTELLIGENCE	ATTRIBUTES	STUDENT ENJOYS	STRATEGIES
MUSICAL -TONE, RHYMING & TIMBRE	PATTERNS OF SOUND NON-VERBAL SOUNDS ENVIRONMENTAL SOUNDS	-IDENTIFYING VARIOUS SOUNDS -MUSIC AND SINGING -"AIR BAND" ACTIVITIES -RHYTHMIC MOVEMENT	-MEMORIZING SONGS -RHYTHMIC ACTIVITIES IN MATH -WRITING MUSIC -MAKING UP RHYMES -USING MUSIC FROM VARIOUS COUNTRIES -DRAMA AND ROLE PLAY USING MUSIC
BODILY-KINESTHETIC -USE OF THE BODY & HANDS	MOVEMENT TO EXPRESS IDEAS & EMOTIONS KNOWLEDGE OF BODY IN SPACE USE OF LARGE & FINE MOTOR SKILLS	-ACTING -PHYSICAL ACTIVITIES -BODY LANGUAGE -DANCES & RHYTHMIC ACTIVITIES -GAMES SUCH AS CHARADES	-PHYSICAL ACTIVITIES - MOVEMENT WHILE WORKING -DANCE & BODY LANGUAGE -ACTING OUT ACTIVITIES -GAMES & SPORTS
NATURALIST - THE ENVIRONMENT	UNDERSTANDING THE NATURAL WORLD APPRECIATING RELATIONSHIPS AMONG LIVING THINGS RECOGNITION OF NATURAL EVENTS & CYCLES.	-CHANGES IN NATURE -WORKING WITH NATURAL MATERIALS -LEARNING ABOUT LIVING THINGS -EXPLORING THE OUTDOORS -OUTDOORS IN GENERAL	-PLAN OUTDOOR ACTIVITIES -REVITALIZE A SECTION OF OUTDOOR WORLD - PLANTS & ANIMALS IN CLASSROOM -TEACH USING NATURAL MATERIALS

INTRAPERSONAL
 	
-UNDERSTANDING
  OTHERS
	NOTICING OTHERS
	
	UNDERSTANDING
	  MOODS
	
	UNDERSTANDING
	  INTERACTIONS OF
	  OTHERS
		-LISTENING TO
		  OTHERS
		
		-MAKING FRIENDS
		
		-WORKING IN A TEAM
		
		-COMING TO
		AGREEMENT
		
		-MEDIATING FOR
		  OTHERS
			-COOPERATIVE
			  MODEL
			
			-USE PEER TUTORS
			
			-PLAN GROUP
			  ASSIGNMENTS
			
			-DEVELOP
			INTERDEPENDENCY
			
			-USE GROUP PROBLEM
			  SOLVING
			
			-USE BRAINSTORMING

INTERPERSONAL
 	
-SELF-KNOWLEDGE
	UNDERSTANDING
	YOUR MOODS
	
	UNDERSTANDING
	YOUR
	MOTIVATIONS
	
	UNDERSTANDING
	  WHAT INFLUENCES
	  YOU
	
	DEVELOPING OWN
	  GOALS
		-SETTING PERSONAL
		  GOALS
		
		-THINKING THROUGH
		  ASSIGNMENTS
		
		-MONITORING SELF-
		  PROGRESS
		
		-MONITORING OWN
		  MOODS & FEELINGS
			-INDIVIDUALIZATION
			
			-PERSONAL GOAL
			  SETTING
			
			-REFLECTION TIME
			
			-SELF-PACED
			  ASSIGNMENTS
			
			-ASSIGNMENT CHOICE
			
			-FEEDBACK
			
			-JOURNALS

LEARNING STYLES

Ms Desjardins' grade six classroom is a busy place with children here and there working busily on mathematics. Ms Desjardins is in front of a chalkboard with 19 girls and boys grouped in front of her with texts open. She is introducing them to the mysteries of taxes and doing some examples on the board. John, a boy with blonde hair, a cheery smile, and a hearing aid watches Ms Desjardins as she speaks. He frowns a bit as the microphone she wears accidently hits her copy of the text. To the window side of the room where sunlight streams in sit the "sunny seven" who love the brightness and say it does them good. Right up close to Ms Desjardins is Monica who can be a handful and tends to wander off task easily. In the opposite rear of the room a group of 6 sit at a large table and converse in twos as they cooperatively work out tax problems Ms Desjardins found in a book on basic accounting. Their mentor, Mrs. Hung, a retired bookkeeper, moves from group to group listening and saying a few words.

Off in a private corner lolling on a huge cushion is Fausia. She works her calculator and neatly prints the answers to multiplication problems in the exercise book on the floor in front of her. Beside her Ann, her friend, sits in her wheelchair putting together shapes of two, three, and four blocks following illustrations drawn on a flipchart by Max. Max is a dropout from the local high school. He is doing community service after trying to wire a blue 95 Chevy without realizing a patrol car was passing by. He assists Ann and works with other students as required.

From behind a privacy screen comes a low hum of background music as four other students play monopoly and each tries to take over the world of finance. The rising level of their conversation lowers suddenly as Serge, one of the group of 19 tells them to "Keep it down, you guys". As he returns to his seat Mr. Finnegan, the inclusion support teacher, comes in the room and crosses over to check on how Ann and Max are doing. He sits down and gives Max quick instructions on how to help Ann use her symbol board to indicate the number of blocks in an illustration before taking on the next one. He says, "Push her a bit Max. You're being too soft and she is taking advantage of you. She won't break, will you Ann?".

This scenario is imaginary only in so far as the words actually used to get some quiet from the monopoly players were not quite as polite as recorded. It was a classroom operating on an individualized program approach with students grouped for instruction according to their needs and ability levels. As in all such classrooms, most of the students were at about a similar level, a number were working further along in the curriculum, and a number were at earlier points. One or two were at quite earlier stages, but all were working away at mathematics in one way or another. If you wanted to be fancy, you would say something such as "A parallel curriculum approach was being implemented". This flexible, general method is found in many inclusive classrooms.

Three adults were in the classroom: the teacher who planned and coordinated all program activities; a community volunteer who loved math and came in every Tuesday and Thursday morning to help in three classrooms rather than going to the senior citizens' centre; and Max, who was discovering that some kids had bigger problems than his, and that he could help them. A fourth adult, Mr. Finnegan, visited the class often to plan with Ms Desjardins, to check on individual progress, and to teach individuals and groups.

It was also a classroom which paid attention to individual learning styles. Go back over the scenario and see if you can find how Ms Desjardins:

- Organized social groupings of different sizes.
- Allowed for individual learning.
- Provided considerable structure for some and less for others.
- Used a games approach for students who enjoyed competition and could monitor themselves.
- Allowed for different levels of lighting.
- Arranged for differing levels of noise.
- Provided for auditory and visual needs.
- Provided alternate forms of demonstrating knowledge.

Ms Desjardins agrees with Thomas De Bello (1989, p. 1) who considers the concept of learning styles to be:

Perhaps the most vital development in education today.

It is a concept which has great affinity to inclusive education. Both call for classrooms structured on different needs. Students learn in the most effective way for them at their level of knowledge. The idea has a natural logic for teachers who see that students vary in the ways they learn. It makes sense to those who see different learning styles and needs in children.

You have your own learning style and so have I. In some ways you and I are different as day and night in how we approach some learning tasks and try to figure out how to complete them. Working and learning in ways that feel right and make sense to you is the natural order of things, an order which can be used to make learning more powerful and pleasing.

> **Learning styles definitely calls for a learner centered approach to teaching.**

One thing you have to watch for, though, is not to require your students to learn through your style. Teachers have always known that different learners have different ways of learning. That knowledge has been subjugated to an approach to teaching which requires learners to learn through the teacher's teaching style, which tends to be patterned on how the teacher learns best. The student is not the centre of the classroom under this approach, the teacher is. In far too many classrooms today that remains the case. Many teachers have a set way of teaching based on their own styles of learning. This is a certain recipe for ensuring that some students in your class, particularly those with more marked learning needs, will not learn as well as they could.

In fact, that approach contributed to the advent of special education with its characteristics of removal of students from regular classrooms and separation of children from their peers. When teachers discovered a wider range of students in their classrooms as society began to make school attendance requisite, and as more students who learned differently entered school, teachers also discovered that the teacher centred model did not work well with all. These learners were deemed to be inefficient and unresponsive. They were seen as not possessing the skills necessary for the traditional classroom. The answer was to send them elsewhere, to group them with like others, and for them to be taught by magician teachers who knew the proper incantations to cure their learning needs and return them to the regular class. As we know now, the magic didn't work, the incantations didn't take, the kids were not cured of their challenges, and special education did not fulfill the early potential educators saw for it.

This is not to say that the teachers in special situations were not good teachers, and did not do their very best. The special class and special school teachers I know are solid professionals and work hard. I know I did my best when I taught in special education, and I know that almost any teacher works in the best interest of the student. It does, however, mean to me that the best sounding solution was tried, but it did not work as well as was hoped. Segregation of students on a regular basis is not the answer to special needs which we thought it would be.

> **We have witnessed a turnaround in our approach to teaching in recent years.**

Now the favoured approach is said to be student centred and collaborative, rather than teacher centred. I say "Is said to be", because I do not believe that the education system has changed all that much when it comes to students with challenging needs. If it has, why do so many school systems maintain elaborate special education structures? Why are so many children bussed out of their communities at great expense to be educated in a system we know does not do much for them academically, and, by its design of grouping with like others, can do little for them socially? The idea of student centred education is denied by the fact that teachers work diligently to move out children who do not achieve well under the way teachers run their classrooms. The curriculum is supposed to be seamless, but it is provided with huge seams by our lockstep graded system of education. Children who are not seen to fit the teacher centred mould challenge teachers to do more than manage classrooms and to actually get around to thoughtful, individually focused teaching.

Now, of course, I am not talking about all teachers and all classrooms. I am not even talking about how many teachers could and would teach all comers, even if they were given the support and freedom to do so. There is little point to castigating teachers who are struggling to do their best, though sometimes hampered by lack of leadership, by inadequate teacher preparation for inclusion, and by other dynamics. I am convinced that the majority of teachers want to be inclusive, but are not certain how to.

This book presents some of the basic concepts and strategies of inclusive teaching. It presents a view that all children are learners who should learn together to get the most from education and to prepare for positive future relationships. It is based firmly on proven practice, on a positive philosophy about learners and teachers, and on supportive research. Specifically, it is based on larger and smaller instructional strategies which work. One of the larger is the concept of learning styles.

THE THEORY

Learning style theory is new even though the idea of individual differences in learning has been known for a long time. Interest in learning style began in earnest during the 1960's and 1970's. From that time to this a number of definitions and theories have been advanced. Whereas definitions vary, one which is accepted by many is that offered by the Learning Styles Task Force of the National Association of Secondary School Principals (Keefe & Monk, 1989).

Learning style is the characteristic cognitive, affective and psychological behaviors that serve as relatively stable indicators of how learners perceive, interact with, and respond to the learning environment.

As noted, there are a number of theories of what learning style is. It is not my intention to review all of them here. For those who wish to pursue this topic in depth, references are provided: (Biggs, 1979; Entwhistle, 1981; Gregorc, 1984; Hill, 1976; Hunt, 1979; Keefe & Monk, 1989; Kolb, 1981; Letteri, 1980; McCarthy, 1981). For the purposes of this book, it may be most productive to provide an outline of an approach to learning style easily grasped by most teachers, and one most easily put into practice. It is also one which I have seen used in various inclusive classrooms to the benefit of all students, both those with and those without disabilities.

Dunn and Dunn

Rita and Kenneth Dunn developed a multidimensional concept of learning style. In my experience their ideas apply well to the classroom and well to the home environment. Their four initial dimensions, augmented by a fifth suggested by De Bello (1989), and the factors associated with each are:

1. **Environment: sound, light, temperature, formal or informal surroundings.**
2. **Emotional: motivation, persistence, responsibility, structure.**
3. **Sociological: pairs, teams, groups, peer group, individual, adult oriented, varied.**
4. **Physical: perceptual preference, need for intake, time of day/night energy levels, mobility preferences.**
5. **Psychological: thinking style, internal or external control.**

Dunn and Dunn see the individual as varying across all five dimensions. If the teacher can discover the preferences of children in the classroom, the environmental, emotional, sociological, physical, and psychological factors of the learning situation can be arranged to provide the individual with the most powerful opportunity for learning. The teacher quickly will realize that many children share preferences and can be grouped for instruction on a logical basis. It is not necessary to develop a totally unique instructional program for every child. However, if a teacher chooses not to pay attention to the learning styles of students, a choice has been made to teach in a hit and miss fashion; in a way which will benefit some students, but will definitely lessen the learning of others.

Dunn, Dunn, and Price (1989) developed a Learning Style Inventory to provide an individual learning style description from elementary through secondary school. Perrin (1984) extended the Dunn et al. work below grade three. Accompanying their descriptive information are ideas that will provide the teacher with the broad strokes of an individual program. My experience is that a thoughtful teacher is quite able to extend the use of these ideas to learners of a wide range of ability levels.

LEARNING STYLES AND STUDENTS WITH SPECIAL NEEDS

Special needs is a generic term for a range of students with widely varying abilities and challenges to their learning. One of the concerns teachers voice is that they fear that the instructional strategies they have at hand will not be sufficiently strong to meet the range of needs which students exhibit. In fact, as the teaching efficacy literature states, and as many teachers have learned, the qualities for teacher effectiveness in terms of instructional strategies are the same for all students, regardless of special needs (Larrivee, 1985). Good teaching for the majority of kids is basically good teaching for all kids.

Learners are learners are learners.

No matter what label we attach to children, their overwhelming similarities deny the differences on which society often focuses. Children are more alike than they are unalike.

It is obvious to anyone who looks that, whereas some children find reading, or math, or physical education, or any other area of learning to be easy, others find the same area to be challenging. When the degree of challenge reaches a certain point, which no-one is able to specify with confidence, no matter how many tests we run, the traditional education system begins to assign labels. After that, we focus on the areas of challenge and begin to define learners by their categories of need. That is how we came up with the population of learners in special education. It is a system based on the negative interpretation of difference.

<table>
<tr><td>

Someone once cried out
"Vive la difference".
Teachers should cry it out too.

</td><td>

I prefer positive interpretations of difference. Education is a profession based on optimism. Negativism is a barrier to appreciating children and teaching well. As Judith Snow (1992, p. 110) says:

</td></tr>
</table>

Each person has a variety of ordinary and extraordinary gifts. The people who we call handicapped are people who are missing some typical ordinary gifts. However, such people also have a variety of other ordinary and extraordinary gifts capable of stimulating interaction and meaning in others.

Among these gifts is the fact that people labeled as special, or disabled, or handicapped, or challenged learn as other people learn. In the sense of the learning style framework of Dunn and Dunn, all learners have environmental, emotional, sociological, physical, and psychological preferences. These can be seen as gifts. Teachers can use these gifts to maximize learning. It really is as straightforward as that. No magic. Just using good teaching ideas with all learners.

Some will argue that there is a qualitative difference in the learning of people with special needs. I agree that different people can learn different amounts of math, or reading, or ballet. However, I do not see that as a reason to separate friend from friend, child from child, peer from peer. We cannot argue successfully that a qualitative difference exists in the learning of different people. How we approach learning and the value of that learning is not dependent on how much curriculum we can master, or even on the curriculum being addressed.

**We all may need different strategies,
and bring different gifts to the table of learning,
but the quality of our learning is not less
because we learn differently than does someone else.**

The mistaken focus on the quantity of learning characteristic of some governments and some educators, rather than on the quality of learning, is one which separates child from child, child from family, and child from community.

Learning style is one approach through which teachers and parents may come to see the commonality of quality of learning among all learners, and thence bring children together. Learning best in a quiet environment does not depend on whether or not one is reading a classic novel or decoding a first word. Feeling confident while learning under teacher guidance is not dependent on subject matter. Preference for learning with others is the same whether one is writing up a group project on the Inca civilization or contributing to the finished product by collating and stapling it. It is possible, however, for teachers and parents to arrange the learning situation to take advantage of the gifts of learning style. The next discussion gives some ideas.

CONTEXTUALIZING LEARNING STYLES

Learning styles is like any other major strategy in operating a classroom. It is something you do to improve the conditions of learning for your students, but is only one of a number of major strategies drawn from background theory on learning. It should not be the only thing you do, and it should not be done by you alone.

Teaching and learning are social activities. You may decide to try out certain aspects of learning styles, but I suggest you talk to your students about what you plan to do. Part of your teaching task is to develop the self-awareness of your students. Chatting with them about the idea of learning styles consulting them about general changes you are considering, enlisting their support in creating and monitoring change are all ways to increase their self-knowledge and their understanding of others. Another suggestion is not to implement anything to which students react negatively. Any strategy will fail if the person at the receiving end doesn't like it. Always check with the group and the individual on strategies. Your students are an integral part of the planning.

I have found that students generally are interested in the idea of learning styles. When you first introduce the concept, many will jump in, cooperate, and work to implement changes. There is a "halo" effect to a new and intriguing idea. However, interest will wane for many after a time. This happens due to the natural lessening of interest in something once it becomes familiar, and to the fact that most of your students will not notice any particular effect of the changes on them. There may be a real long-term effect, but it is gradual for most, who are generally capable, all-around learners with average to good basic capacity.

But in an inclusive classroom you also have a number of learners who need help in organizing their learning and making the most of their environment. In my view this is where the value of learning styles comes in. The learning of these students tends to be less than what is possible. Our regular classroom strategies are not as effective in reaching them as we might wish. For these students small changes may have meaningful effect.

Students with challenges to their learning will not be cured of them through use of learning styles. The classroom is not a hospital for broken learners where pedagogical operations are performed. The needs of learners with disabilities are part of their being. Though needs may be reduced or gotten around through the use of some strategy, they tend not to disappear completely. Thoughtfully implemented changes to the environment will do a great deal to enable these learners to reveal more of their potential and partake in learning more powerfully. It is for these learners that learning style theory and practice have the greatest meaning.

ENVIRONMENTAL FACTORS

Research indicates that environmental factors affect up to 40 per cent of students (Dunn, Beaudy, & Klavas, 1989). Teachers and parents are able to arrange factors such as sound, light, and temperature for the benefit of children. The basic idea is that some will prefer background sound as they work. Others will prefer a silent setting. The same for other environmental factors.

Just think for a minute about how you arrange your own environment when you want to study or work on a project. You do certain things because you have learned that that is the way you prefer to learn, the way you feel most comfortable and prepared. If that works for you, why wouldn't it work for others. One example that comes to mind is that of my two youngest children, Adam and Megan. They are both in high school now and doing well. All their school life they have sat in front of the television while doing their homework. I thought this was crazy and that they could not concentrate while the TV was on. They said they could. I hassled them for a long time before it came to me that they were doing well in school. Now I just look at them, shake my head, and assure myself that they really can't learn that way. But I leave them alone. Their grades and the comments of their teachers finally convinced me. They don't learn exactly as I do, but then I don't learn exactly as they do. Sometimes it takes me a long time to see the obvious.

Don't limit anyone by restricting them
to how you prefer to set up your learning environment.

Here are some beginning ideas. Space has been left for you to add others that meet the needs of your particular students.

Differing Levels of Sound

♬   Arrange group and individual learning and study areas.

♬   Use earphones (e.g. Walkman) for individuals.

♬   Seat certain students away from noise of door and windows.

♬   Use rugs or carpets in defined parts of the room.

♬   Place used tennis balls over the feet of chairs and desks.

♬   Alternate active and quiet activities.

♬   Use space dividers as sound buffers.

♬   Use different spaces of school (e.g. hallways, library) for different groups.

♬   _____

♬   _____

♬   _____

♬   _____

♬   _____

DIFFERING LEVELS OF LIGHT

✧   Seat near natural light at windows.

✧   Use adjustable curtains/blinds.

✧   Seat away from light of windows.

✧   Use portable lamps.

✧   Use only selected ceiling lighting.

✧   Turn lights off during day.

✧   _____

✧   _____

✧   _____

✧   _____

✧   _____

DIFFERING FORMAL & INFORMAL SURROUNDINGS

☐   Provide a formal seating area.

☐   Allow for rearrangement of desks.

☐   Provide a casually designed area with sofa, soft chair, rugs.

☐   Provide straight backed chairs.

☐   Provide cushions.

☐   Provide for small study group areas.

☐   Use learning centres.

☐   Set aside special space for special activities.

- ☐   _____
- ☐   _____
- ☐   _____
- ☐   _____
- ☐   _____

Differing Temperature Levels

- ✿   Maintain consistent average temperature.
- ✿   Encourage students to have extra sweater or cap available.
- ✿   Plan seating taking windows, doors, and air conditioners into consideration.
- ✿   Arrange for small portable fans.
- ✿   Seat students near windows.
- ✿   Provide work areas near heating units.
- ✿   _____
- ✿   _____
- ✿   _____
- ✿   _____
- ✿   _____

EMOTIONAL FACTORS

Students respond on emotional levels as well as on cognitive levels. Without a positive emotional atmosphere in a classroom learning is problematic, more so for some students than for others. Though it is challenging to realize and act on the fact that different learners approach the same learning situations individually, it is part of the teacher's responsibility to plan strategies to take advantage of, or to bolster, the emotional state of the learner. As Jere Brophy (1987), one of the big names in the psychology of how children learn, says:

Students are more likely to want to learn when they appreciate the value of the classroom activities and when they believe they will succeed if they apply reasonable effort.

Here the factors of importance are motivation, persistence, and responsibility. Remember, different strokes work for different folks.

Self - Motivated

- ➢ Negotiate individual/group contracts.
- ➢ Self-directed activities.
- ➢ Choice of when to undertake tasks.
- ➢ Teach goal-setting and self-appraisal.
- ➢ Choice of free-time activities.
- ➢ _____
- ➢ _____
- ➢ _____
- ➢ _____
- ➢ _____

Low Motivation

- ➢ Focus on interests to promote meaningful environment.
- ➢ Work in groups on interactive tasks.
- ➢ Stimulate self and interpersonal competition under equitable conditions.
- ➢ Pair off with motivated partner.

> Make use of novelty.

> Use group evaluation techniques.

> Use game-like strategies.

> Vary social setting, nature of instruction, type of task.

> _____

> _____

> _____

> _____

> _____

Persistence

> Assign pair or group activities of various lengths.

> Set time for activities and keep class informed as time passes.

> Create opportunities for unstructured time.

> Monitor from a distance.

> _____

> _____

> _____

> _____

> _____

Low Persistence

> Link with more persistent student.

> Monitor from nearby.

> Break down tasks into short periods.

> Use positive reinforcement (but try to avoid operant conditioning).

➢ _____
➢ _____
➢ _____
➢ _____
➢ _____

Responsible

➢ Reinforce positive nature of this characteristic.

➢ Provide opportunities for responsibility.

➢ Monitor from a distance.

➢ Vary between self-directed and teacher-directed activities.

➢ _____

➢ _____

➢ _____

➢ _____

➢ _____

Low Responsibility

➢ Reinforce completion of tasks.

➢ Use timed tasks.

➢ Keep chart on task completion,

➢ Pair with more responsible student.

➢ Monitor from nearby and frequently.

➢ Make tasks explicit.

➢ Use games strategy.

➢ Include competition elements.

➢ _____

➢ _____

➢ _____

➢ _____

➢ _____

SOCIOLOGICAL FACTORS

As was said earlier, "Man is a social animal". Our society takes children at a young and tender age and places them in school with other children for periods of 13 years or more. It is normal according to our society, for children to be educated in a diverse social environment with constant guidance from adult strangers called teachers. There is no doubt that social preference has an impact on school achievement. Today's emphasis on teacher-guided cooperative learning, group projects, and other social strategies create opportunities for social collaboration and the development of leadership and interdependence. Group, pair, team, self-orientation, and adult-orientation, or a variety of these social situations, will meet the needs of all learners. As with any set of strategies, variety is the spice of life. Experience will tell you how much variety and how much consistency individual students need to support their learning.

Individual Preference

☺ Arrange work areas for individual work.

☺ Provide for individual work in private space.

☺ Use self-evaluation techniques.

☺ Have a special space for short term needs for privacy.

☺ Lay out clearly the conditions for evaluation of individual projects.

☺ Design lessons with individual and group activities.

☺ _____

☺ _____

☺ _____

☺ _____

☺ _____

Preference for One Partner

☺ Arrange desks, working spots for pairs.

☺ Initiate a buddy system.

☺ Design tasks to permit work in pairs.

☺ Set up small team activities.

☺ Use games played by pairs.

☺ _____

☺ _____

☺ _____

☺ _____

☺ _____

Preference for Groups

☺ Use tables or groups of desks for working areas.

☺ Initiate a group evaluation system.

☺ Develop a form listing student names and task responsibilities by groups.

☺ Use group games.

☺ _____

☺ _____

☺ _____

☺ _____

Adult Preference

☺ Offer teacher-directed activities.

☺ Routinely monitor individual and group activities.

☺ Set up an adult coaching system for tasks.

☺ Set up procedure for student to consult with teacher as work progresses.

☺ Have student work with teacher on evaluation of work.

☺ Encourage parents to support homework activities.

☺ _____

☺ _____

☺ _____

☺ _____

☺ _____

PHYSICAL FACTORS

Schools have not done a strong job of addressing the physical preferences of students. Traditionally, the physical set-up of classrooms and work schedules were arranged on the apparent belief that children were merely miniature adults and should be treated as such. This is the "Children should be seen but not heard." view of development. The child is just a little adult in being. This view of the child has been referred to as homuncular theory. It is an old theory that says the child was simply an adult in being and has been discarded. Teachers must watch out that education does not revive this theory through the way that children are taught in some classrooms.

More and more can be and should be done to address individual learning styles in the physical sense. We accept without much argument that there are auditory learners, visual learners, and auditory/visual learners. There may even be tactile learners, those who learn best by the hands-on approach. If we think about ourselves or those we know well, we understand that some people are best in the morning, others in the afternoon, and others late at night. We understand without thinking much about it that some people need to be active as they work out an idea, while others need to be quiet and still. For others still, a snack seems to facilitate learning. Research supports these understandings and even others (Dunn, Beaudry, Klavas, 1989; Lembke, 1985; Semple, 1982). Advocates of learning styles propose that our understandings now be applied in the classroom.

Auditory Preference

- Instruct using verbal mode.
- Permit inter-student discussion of work.
- Use presentations, debates, drama for assignments.
- Use videos and films.
- Invite speakers.
- _____
- _____
- _____
- _____
- _____

Visual Preference

- Use overhead to support instruction.

☺   Make use of television, videos, films.

☺   Use chalkboard notes and generally include pictures, maps, etc. in lessons.

☺   Prepare lesson notes as student guides.

☺   Include reading tasks.

☺   _____

☺   _____

☺   _____

☺   _____

☺   _____

Preference for Food Intake

☺   Allow snacks during the day.

☺   Keep a stock of nutritional snacks in the classroom.

☺   Allow gum chewing.

☺   Ensure that all children have had breakfast.

☺   Ensure that all children have lunch.

☺   _____

☺   _____

☺   _____

☺   _____

☺   _____

Time Preference

☺   Observe student work patterns to determine time of day preference.

☺   Ask students what time of day is best for them.

☺   Conduct problem-solving activities during best times.

☺ Develop a flexible timetable for dealing with program content.

☺ Provide for catch up time daily at student's choice of time.

☺ _____

☺ _____

☺ _____

☺ _____

☺ _____

Preference for Movement

☺ Permit quiet out-of-seat participation.

☺ Permit degree of quiet individual movement.

☺ Plan for hands on activities.

☺ Arrange for some out-of-classroom activities.

☺ Include short exercise periods daily.

☺ Provide for interactive lessons.

☺ _____

☺ _____

☺ _____

☺ _____

☺ _____

PSYCHOLOGICAL FACTORS

The big areas here are global/analytic preferences, impulsive/reflective preferences, and left/right hermisphericity. Some students naturally work from the big picture. Others like to go at tasks step by step. Some jump right into things. Others will try to figure out how to approach a job before they begin. Some like facts and figures, words and details. Music, art, and how things move in space and time are favoured by still others. These are all ways that students operate on a routine basis. Knowing the general strategies of your students will assist you in setting up your learning opportunities to match their learning styles.

Rather than laying out various categories of ideas here, I have opted to present a few general points. If you want to emphasize a certain understanding of the psychology of learning, I suggest that you look for a useful review. A good many positions on the areas noted above may be located by looking up the references given earlier in this section. My preferred approach is to think of learners as leaning to innovative, or analytic, or common sense, or dynamic styles. The chart at the end of this section notes aspects under this approach.

- Be flexible in setting out how tasks are to be done.
- Suggest alternative ways to approach activities.
- Provide time for thought.
- Check understanding and progress of those who begin right away.
- Give individual assistance to those who seem to be hesitating.
- Provide a variety of activities.
- Break tasks down into component parts as well as giving the whole.
- Have plenty of resources available.
- Pair up different kinds of learners.
- Create situations calling for intuitive and rational understanding.
- Provide both verbal and visuo-spatial material.
- Provide opportunity for both imaginative and deductive talk.
- Value both objective and subjective thought processes.
- _____
- _____
- _____
- _____
- _____

SUMMARY OF DUNN AND DUNN FACTORS

All of these ideas work with some learners. Some are effective for many, some for a few. Some are effective but then are less necessary as the students grows older. Recall the opening scenario of Ms Desjardins' classroom. She did not attempt to implement a huge number of learning style strategies, but merely selected a few and implemented them. In chatting with her I found that she began slowly with a focus on her students with the greatest degrees of challenge. Then she moved on to other students and built up a routine which she now adjusts as necessary. She kept her students aware of what she was trying to do and they assisted her with suggestions. All along the way she had the help of Mr. Finnegan who had studied exceptionality and had experience supporting teachers in regular classrooms.

For teachers who think about how their students learn, ways can be found to try out strategies and then select those which appear most beneficial and practical. Planned implementation does not interfere with the regular program for other students and the class keeps moving. Of course, it depends on a teacher who is willing to try new ideas and try them for long enough to see how they work. Predeciding that a particular strategy will not work or is too difficult to implement is a sign of a teacher deciding not to do something that may help a student. Professionals know that positive change may require innovation and effort. Fortunately, learning strategies of the type Dunn and Dunn suggest comfortably fit into almost all classrooms. And teachers already know most of the ideas.

ASSESSING LEARNING STYLES

One sticking point for some teachers is "How do I determine what my student's learning style is?". Fortunately, the answer is relatively simple. There are two ways to go. One is to administer an inventory of learning styles. The second is more informal and personal. It is to observe your student as she learns, to ask how she learns best, and to talk to the parents or previous teachers about preferred learning style.

If you elect to take the formal route, you can use the Learning Style Inventory (LSI) developed by Dunn, Dunn, and Price (1989) for grades three through high school. For earlier grades you can try Perrin's Primary Version of the LSI (1984). These instruments contain True/False questions which probe environmental, emotional, sociological, physical, and psychological areas. The student (or an informed other in the case of some highly challenged students) answers the questions and a scoring system tells you which factors are important to the individual. Your Mr. Finnegan should be able to help you find the commercially published LSI.

I find the less formal route more to my taste. The base is observation of a student. There are a variety of simple observational guides available. Again, your Mr. Finnegan can help. What is called for is routine observation for a minute or two at a time as students work on different tasks in differing settings, and making brief notes to remind you of what you saw. You may even decide to design your own guide. You know enough about the five areas now to develop a short instrument to fit your teaching situation. As an alternative, I have added something I designed at the end of this chapter.

A productive way of obtaining information about your student is to use a guide for your own observations, but also to use it to guide discussions with those who know her well. It is amazing how insightful students, parents, siblings, and friends can be. On second thought, it is not all that amazing. Anyone who spends time with another person naturally picks up a lot of information about that person. Sometimes they don't even know they have the information until someone sits down and asks about it. Using a simple guide as your source for questions can reveal a great deal and provide you with wonderful ideas.

The third part of this informal triangular assessment of someone's learning style involves the student. Ask her how she likes to learn. Again, you can use your observational guide. Even young children know what they prefer in many ways. One of our failings as teachers is that we do not ask often enough when we need information. We tend to depend on ourselves. But as noted earlier on a number of occasions, teaching is a social activity. We may know a great deal as professionals, but that doesn't mean that it hurts to check with others. We may even learn something. Lee Marcus (1977) carried out an interesting little study which makes this point.

Grade nine teachers were given a list of factors and asked to name those which they thought important for each of their students. Then the students were asked which factors were important in their learning. Results showed that teacher and student opinions frequently differed. Where agreement exists, there could easily be important learning. There could be even more important learning where disagreement exists.

Talk to your students! Talk to their families and friends!
Together we are better!

QUICK OBSERVATION OF LEARNING STYLE

Student: _____ Activity: _____

Observer: _____ Date: _____

Circle the appropriate descriptor.

ENVIRONMENT

Sound	Quiet	Background Noise	Doesn't Matter
Light	Low	Bright	Doesn't Matter
Temperature	Cool	Warm	Doesn't Matter
Room Style	Informal	Formal	Doesn't Matter

EMOTIONAL

Motivation	Self	Peer	Adult	Doesn't Matter
Persistence	High	Low	Varies	Doesn't Matter
Responsibility	High	Low	Varies	Doesn't Matter
Structure	High	Medium	Low	Doesn't Matter

SOCIOLOGICAL

Pairs	Prefers	Avoids	Doesn't Matter
Small Peer Group	Prefers	Avoids	Doesn't Matter
Large Peer Group	Prefers	Avoids	Doesn't Matter
Adult Orientation	Prefers	Avoids	Doesn't Matter
Self Orientation	Prefers	Avoids	Doesn't Matter

PHYSICAL

Auditory	**Prefers**	**Avoids**		**Doesn't Matter**
Visual	**Prefers**	**Avoids**		**Doesn't Matter**
Tactile	**Prefers**	**Avoids**		**Doesn't Matter**
Food Intake	**Prefers**	**Avoids**		**Doesn't Matter**
Mobility	**Prefers**	**Avoids**		**Doesn't Matter**
Time	**Early** **Mid-day**	**Afternoon**	**Evening**	**Doesn't Matter**

PSYCHOLOGIAL[1]

Innovative	**Concrete Learner**	**Collaborative**	**Reflective**
	Direct Teaching	**Divergent**	
Analytic	**Details & Facts**	**Direct Teaching**	**Thorough**
	Abstract	**Book Oriented**	
Common Sense	**Hands on**	**Practical**	**Abstract**
	Decision Maker	**Extrovert**	
Dynamic	**Concrete**	**Trial & Error**	**Enthusiastic**
	Likes Case Studies	**Task Variety**	

[1] All 5 characteristics listed under each of the four types of learners are related to that type. Not all need to be circled to place a learner primarily under one type. Learners commonly will display some characteristics under a second or third type. It is the clustering which has meaning.

MY THOUGHTS

I have tried to be straightforward and simple in this book. That probably is because I really do believe inclusion to be simple and straightforward. To me, it is more a matter of our attitude toward students with disabilities and their place in school than it is whether or not we can be inclusive. Of course, being inclusive is easier if we are supported in doing it. But we can make real advances toward inclusion ourselves, just using our own skills as teachers and by working with our students, their parents, and any others who believe children should be with other children. Saying "They won't give us the supports we need, therefore we can't do it" is to turn our backs on something we know is beneficial for all children. Doing what we can with what we have is the most that can be expected of us. This thought is touched on in the first chapter.

A child or adult with a disability is a personal test through which we teachers face our feelings about difference head on. Inclusion is about how we relate to people who look, act, or think differently than do so-called "ordinary" people.

This leads me to my next thought and to the second chapter. Every classroom has a culture. Yours has. Mine has. It speaks to us as professionals and members of the community, and it speaks to what teaching is all about. We and our students can work toward developing a classroom culture where all are accepted and respected, or toward a culture where some are accepted and others have no place. Your choice. My choice.

There is absolutely no doubt but that you will develop a classroom culture. Part of that culture will grow from how much you contribute of yourself.

The next thought is one which teachers struggle with due to the way we have been taught to think about students and the curriculum. Where I live and work right now the curriculum and following it is right at the top of the agenda. If the student cannot meet or exceed the grade three or grade ten curriculum standards laid down for everyone else, the student is devalued and her/his presence in the classroom is questioned. I don't accept this. The learner is more important than the curriculum. Being with others of your age and from your community is more important than the curriculum. In fact, as I write this I am thinking that I am referring to our preoccupation with the academic curriculum. We are forced into forgetting the social/affective curriculum and this is wrong. Both are there to provide the best possible education to all children, and the two curricula must be accessible to all.

The curriculum is not our master.
It is our servant in education.

The next chapter is all about an extension of creating a classroom culture and about making the curriculum accessible. It focuses on the idea that we all are social animals. We live in a society, meet others, love others, like some and dislike some. Our learning takes place in the company of others. Making the most of our classrooms as social microcosms will strengthen them as academic environments. We are meant to be together, to learn about our culture, and to learn the social and academic things that will maximize our abilities, our sense of self, and our contributions to our communities.

We do not need a lengthy and complex treatise to persuade us that we learn
best in the society of others. Separating learner from learner on the assumption
that they will learn better in homogenous groups, denies the reality of what we
teachers know about learning.

These first few thoughts, captured in the first four chapters, suggest a way of thinking about children, difference, education, learning, and teaching. They lead to a series of discussions focused on teaching strategies we know are sound theoretically. These strategies are so well regarded that you find evidence of most or all of them in every decent classroom. We rely on them to teach students in regular classrooms. Well, if you talk to teachers who are known to be inclusive, and if you know any of the literature on inclusion, you also know that these same teaching strategies are the underpinnings of the inclusive approach.

For instance, we know that teachers can help students learn. We know that parents can help and that peers can help, as well as the babysitter or the store manager. All of these can help because there is a social base to cognitive development. In this book I talk about Vygotsky as one person whose theoretical views on this have resulted in ideas for effective teaching. Though we say "theoretical", the ideas are simple.

Learning is a social activity which occurs between the learner and the teacher. The teacher may be a professional, a parent, a peer, or any other person who knows more than does the learner and is able to communicate that knowledge.

I know that not all learners with challenges have the same challenge or the same degree of challenge. There are differences, as there are in every facet of life. For the great majority the degree of challenge is not high and does not present great obstacles for the teacher. Most of us already know how to include these learners, whether we actually do or not. A sampling of strategies for this group and for two other groups, those with somewhat higher degrees of challenges and those with quite high degrees, is given in the *Strategies for Differing Levels of Abilities* chapter. My thought here is that there are ways to include any learner, and these ways are known to us.

The good news is that once teachers decide to work with students with low to high levels of challenge, they find it quite possible. There are teachers working with all types of needs every day in schools not that far distant from you.

An obvious bias in my ideas is that teaching and learning are social activities. I have extended this idea in a discussion of how to work collaboratively with others in support of your students. I've heard an old saying that "Many hands make light work", and this applies to teaching inclusively. One thing that we know is that being inclusive is different than traditional practice in that it calls for a team approach. The team will vary depending of the needs and strengths of any student, but parents, resource teachers, educational assistants, volunteers, and principals figure strongly. Any classroom is a busy place. Sharing the work and responsibilities of the classroom is one of the ways to make an inclusive approach work.

Inclusion and the diversity of ability of the students in a classroom means that the traditional model requires adjustment. Inclusion suggests working in teams, and cooperation, and collaboration not taught in teacher preparation programs in the past.

One of the major concerns teachers have relative to inclusion is that they will not have enough time to do it well. That is certainly worth spending a thought on. And I have. Lots and lots of thought and lots and lots of talks with teachers, parents, principals, and persons with disabilities. What I have found is that time is a concern, but that there are ways to reduce the concern. The teacher must not steal time from the majority of students in order to attend to the needs of the included student. First of all, the student cannot learn as fast as you want to teach in many cases. Most students who are challenged are considered so because experience has proven that they learn at their own pace. No matter how you try to push the student ahead, it doesn't work. You will be wasting your time and frustrating both the student and yourself. Secondly, if the time is needed to attend to the student, use a peer, educational assistant, or a volunteer to do what you do not have time to do. Another time concern is that around planning. This calls for more creativity, but collaboration is at least part of the solution here as well. Some ideas are given for this in the chapter on *Time*.

These types of ideas may not solve every time problem, but they will lessen them.

The last two chapters in the book are really one thought. There are major strategies which you can use to make the most of everyone's abilities and to meet their needs. These will not "cure" any student, but, in concert with respect and acceptance of all students, and a student centered approach to curriculum, they will give everyone an equitable chance. They are the use of Multiple Intelligences and Learning Styles as broad approaches to your organization of the classroom. Both regard all students as having many things to offer in a classroom and many ways of offering them. They also fit in well with teachers' intuitive understanding of how students learn - all students.

I hope you enjoyed this book as much as I enjoyed writing it. If you would like to correspond with me, find me on E-mail at gbunch@edu.yorku.ca.

Marsha Forest and Jack Pearpoint, who are inclusive educators and who began Inclusion Press, asked me where my thoughts came from, specifically what books might have contributed to forming them. They asked me to mention them.

Here is a short list of those few pieces of writing which I now understand have had effect on me over the years. In every case I did not realize it at the time, but I found myself thinking of them, of certain phrases, certain ideas, as I entered more and more into inclusive philosophy and practice. In a sense, it has been a type of collaboration among people who mostly never meet - the author who puts her/his ideas into print and the person who reads them.

The first is Richard Brautigan's *Rommel Drives on Deep into Egypt* (Dell Publishing). It is a small book of poems by a 1960's California hippie who committed suicide in the early 1980's. One poem in particular pierced me when I first read it. And it still does. Here it is.

The Memoirs of Jesse James

I remember all those thousands of hours
that I spent in grade school watching the clock,
    waiting for recess or lunch or to go home.
Waiting: for anything but school.
My teachers could easily have ridden with Jesse James
    for all the time they stole from me.

The next is by Albert Cullum (Harlin Quist Incorporated) an elementary school teacher. The contents are fine, but they are not why the book surfaces in my mind with startling frequency when I think about teaching, teachers, children, and inclusion. It is the title which hit me.

The Geranium on the Window Sill Just Died
But the Teacher Went Right On

I guess I must prefer small books because the next is really just a pamphlet of 21 pages by Marsha Forest. The title is *It's About Relationships* (Inclusion Press) and is a chat by Marsha about the need for us all to build relationships to heal ourselves and to heal our communities. The thread Marsha draws through the book is inclusion.

Finally, I get to two books which people might call "serious". They stuck in my mind more than my heart, which is where the first three went. But like those three, they have had a great deal to do with how I think about all students and about learning in schools. One, *Toward a Theory of Instruction* (Harvard University Press), is by the great American psychologist Jerome Bruner. The other, *Thought and Language* (The MIT Press), is by the wonderful Russian psychologist Lev Vygotsky whose works we could not read about in the West for years because the cold war was on. Bruner talks about the power that young children bring to the act of learning and the restrictions schools put on that learning. Vygotsky talks about the interplay of language and thought in the stimulation of intelligence. Neither talks about inclusion, but their thoughts are directly applicable. Heavy reads, but wow!

I was surprised when I sat down to think of what books had had effect on me that there were so few. I am a reader, and a teacher, and now a professor of education and I have read thousands. But only in a few instances did certain lines leap off the page and smack me on the forehead. And only a few quietly slipped into my soul and became a part of me. I'm glad they did.

What are the things that have formed your views about children, teachers, and schools and how they come together? Where does your thinking come from?

REFERENCES

Armstrong, T. (1994). <u>Multiple intelligences in the classroom</u>. Alexandria, VA: Association for Supervision and Curriculum Development.

Biggs, J. (1979). Individual differences in study progress and the quality of learning outcomes. <u>Higher Education, 18</u>, 384-394.

Brophy, J. (1987, October). Synthesis of research on strategies for motivating students to learn. <u>Educational Leadership</u>, 40-48.

Bunch, G. (1989). The need for redefinition. In J. Pearpoint, M. Forest, and J. Snow (Eds.), <u>The inclusion papers: Strategies to make inclusion work</u> (pp.111-113). Toronto: Inclusion Press.

Bunch, G. (1995). <u>Kids, disabilities and regular classrooms: An annotated bibliography of selected childrens' literature</u>. Toronto: Inclusion Press

Bunch, G., Lupart, J., & Brown, M. (1997). <u>Resistance and acceptance: Teacher attitudes to inclusion of students with disability</u>. Toronto: Faculty of Education, York University

Bunch, G. & Valeo, A. (1997). <u>Inclusion: Recent research</u>. Toronto: Inclusion Press.

Checkley, K. (1997). The first seven ... and the eighth. <u>Educational Leadership</u>, 8-13.

DeBello, T. C., (1989). <u>Comparison of eleven major learning style models: Validity of instrumentation and the reasons behind them</u>. (ERIC Documentation Service No. ED 312 093).

Dunn, R., Beaudry, J. S., & Klavas, A. (1989, March). Survey of research on learning styles. <u>Educational Leadership</u>, 50-58.

Dunn. R., Dunn, K., & Price, G. (1989). <u>Learning Style Inventory (LSI): An inventory for the identification of how individuals in grades 3 through 12 prefer to learn</u>. Lawrence, Kansas: Price Systems, Inc.

Earl. L., & Cousins, J. B., (1996). <u>Classroom assessment: Changing the face, facing the change</u>. Scarborough, ON: Allyn and Bacon Canada.

Entwhistle, N. (1981). <u>Styles of learning and teaching</u>. Chichester, UK: Wiley.

Gardner, H. (1983). <u>Frames of mind</u>. N.Y: Basic Books

Gardner, H. (1987). Beyond the IQ: Education and human development. Harvard Educational Review, 57(2), 187-193.

Gelb-Shuhendler, J. (1998). The diagnostic assessment process: Making the paradigm shift by uniting theory and practice. Unpublished Master's Research Project, Toronto: Faculty of Education, York University.

Gregorc, A. F. (1984, winter). Styles as a symptom: A phenomenological perspective. Theory Into Practice, 23, 51-55.

Hahn, H. (1988). The politics of physical differences: Disability and discrimination. Journal of Social Issues, 44(1), 39-47.

Hill, J. E. (1976). The educational sciences. Bloomfield Hills, NJ: Oakland Community College Press.

Hunt, D. (1979). Learning style and student need: An introduction to conceptual level. In Student learning styles: Diagnosing and prescribing programs. Reston, VA: National Association of Secondary School Principals.

Keefe, J. W., & Monk, J. S. (1989). Learning style profile manual. Reston, VA: National Association of Secondary School Principals.

Kolb, D. A. (1981). Experiential learning theory and the Learning Style Inventory. A reply to Friedman and Stumpf. Academy of Management Review, 6(2), 289-296.

Krantz, G., & Whitbread, K. (Eds.). (1996). Multiple intelligences in the classroom. The Inclusion Notebook, 1(1), 4.

Larrivee, B. (1985). Effective teaching for successful mainstreaming. NY: Longman.

Lembke, B. (1985). The dynamics of learning style as a viable teaching paradigm. Unpublished manuscript. (ERIC Documentation Reproduction Service No. 260-794).

Letteri, C. A. (1980). Cognitive profile: Basic determinants of cognitive achievement. Journal of Educational Resource, 73, 195-199.

Marcus, L. (1977, April). How teachers view student learning styles. NAASP Bulletin, 61(408), 112-114.

McCarthy, B. (1980). The 4MAT system: Teaching to learning styles with right/left mode techniques. Barrington, IL: Excel, Inc.

McCowan, R. R., Driscoll, M., Roop, P., Saklofske, D. H., Kelly, I. W., Schwean, V. L., & Gajadharsingh, J. (1996). Educational psychology: A learner-centered approach to classroom practice. Scarborough, ON: Allyn and Bacon.

Mercer, C. D., Lane, H. B., Jordan, L., Allsopp, D. H., & Eisele, M. R. (1996). Empowering teachers and students with instructional choices in inclusive settings. Remedial and Special Education, 17(4), 226-236.

Perrin, J. (1984). An experimental investigation of the relationships among the learning style profiles of gifted and non-gifted children, selected instructional practice, attitudes, and achievement in problem solving and rote memorization. (Doctoral dissertation, St. John's University, 1990). Dissertation Abstracts International, 46, 342-02A.

Pick, H. L., & Gippenreiter, J. B., (1994). Vygotskian theories of intelligence. In R. J. Sternberg (Ed.), Encyclopedia of human intelligence (pp. 1122-1126). N.Y: Macmillan.

Semple, E. E. (1982). Learning style: A review of the literature. Garrettsville, OH: Garfield Local Schools. (ERIC Document Reproduction Service No. ED 222-477).

Snow, J. (1992). Dreaming, speaking, and creating: What I know about community. In J. Pearpoint, M. Forest, & J. Snow (Eds.), The inclusion papers: Strategies to make inclusion work. Toronto: Inclusion Press.

Sternberg, R. J. (1989). The tyranny of testing. Learning, 60-63.

Sternberg, R. J. (1994, November). Allowing for thinking styles. Educational Leadership, 36-40

Udvari, Solner, A. (1996). Examining teacher thinking: Constructing a process to design curricular adaptations. Remedial and Special Education, 17(4), 245-254.

Valeo, A. (1994). Inclusive education support systems: Teacher and administrator views. Unpublished Masters Research Project, Toronto: Faculty of Education, York University.

INCLUSION PRESS ORDER FORM

24 Thorne Crescent, Toronto, ON Canada M6H 2S5
Tel: 416-658-5363 Fax: 416-658-5067
E-mail: inclusionpress@inclusion.com
WEBSITE: http://www.inclusion.com

Inclusion SPECIAL PACKS...

* PATH IN ACTION PACK $150 + $15 shipping/pack   ____ _____
- 2 Path Training Videos [(Path in Action + Path Training) + Path Workbook]

* All Means All PACK $110 + $10 shipping/pack   ____ _____
- Video: All Means All, plus & book: All My Life's a Circle

* Friendship PACK (1 book + Video) $ 60 + $10 shipping/pack   ____ _____
- [Friendship Video + From Behind the Piano/What's Really Worth Doing]

* Inclusion Classics Videos PACK $ 90 + $12 shipping/pack   ____ _____
- Videos [With a Little Help from My Friends + Kids Belong Together]

* Inclusion Classics Book PACK $ 30 + $7 shipping/pack   ____ _____
- Books [Action for Inclusion + The Inclusion Papers]

* Petroglyphs PACK $ 60 + $10 shipping/pack   ____ _____
- Petroglyphs Book and Video on Inclusion in High Schools - from UNH

* When Spider Webs Unite PACK $ 80 + $10 shipping/pack   ____ _____
- When Spider Webs Unite - Shafik Asante - Book and Video

* The Education Book PACK $ 40 + $7 shipping/pack   ____ _____
- Inclusion: Recent Research & Inclusion: How To - 2 Books - Gary Bunch

* The Community PACK $ 40 + $7 shipping/pack   ____ _____
- Members of Each Other & Celebrating the Ordinary - 2 books - John O'Brien & Connie Lyle O'Brien

Books

	Copies	Total

A Little Book About Person Centered Planning $20 + $5 /1st copy shipping   ____ _____
Edited by John O'Brien & Connie Lyle O'Brien with Forest, Lovett, Mount, Pearpoint, Smull, Snow, and Strully

All My Life's a Circle Expanded Edition- Circles, MAPS & PATH $20 + $5 /1st copy shipping   ____ _____

Path Workbook - 2nd Edition Planning Positive Possible Futures $20 + $5 /1st copy shipping   ____ _____

Celebrating the Ordinary   O'Brien, O'Brien & Jacob $25 + $5 /1st copy shipping   ____ _____

Members of Each Other   John O'Brien & Connie Lyle O'Brien $25 + $5 /1st copy shipping   ____ _____

Action for Inclusion - Classic on Inclusion $20 + $5 /1st copy shipping   ____ _____

The Inclusion Papers - Strategies & Stories $20 + $5 /1st copy shipping   ____ _____

Lessons for Inclusion Curriculum Ideas for Inclusion in Elementary Schools $20 + $5 /1st copy shipping   ____ _____

Inclusion: How To   Essential Classroom Strategies - Gary Bunch $25+ $5 /1st copy shipping   ____ _____

Inclusion: Recent Research   G. Bunch & A. Valeo $25 + $5 /1st copy shipping   ____ _____

Kids, Disabilities Regular Classrooms   Gary Bunch $20 + $5 /1st copy shipping   ____ _____

Reflections on Inclusive Education $15 + $5 /1st copy shipping   ____ _____

Each Belongs - Hamilton Wentworth Catholic School Bd - J. Hansen $20 + $5 /1st copy shipping   ____ _____

From Behind the Piano, by Jack Pearpoint AND **What's Really Worth Doing** by Judith Snow
- Now in ONE Book * $20 + $5 /1st copy shipping   ____ _____

When Spider Webs Unite Community & Inclusion- Shafik Asante $20 + $5 /1st copy shipping   ____ _____

Yes! She Knows She's Here Nicola Schaefer's NEW Book $20 + $5 /1st copy shipping   ____ _____

Dream Catchers & Dolphins Marsha Forest and Jack Pearpoint $20 + $5 /1st copy shipping   ____ _____

It Matters - Lessons from my Son - Janice Fialka $15 + $5 /1st copy shipping   ____ _____

Do You Hear What I Hear? - Janice Fialka & Karen Mikus $15 + $5 /1st copy shipping   ____ _____

The Careless Society - John McKnight $25 + $5 /1st copy shipping   ____ _____

Who Cares - David Schwartz $30 + $5 /1st copy shipping   ____ _____

The All Star Company - Team Building by Nick Marsh $20 + $5 /1st copy shipping   ____ _____

Changes in Latitudes/Attitudes Role of the Inclusion Facilitator $20 + $5 /1st copy shipping   ____ _____

Petroglyphs - Inclusion in High School from UNH $20 + $5 /1st copy shipping   ____ _____

Treasures - from UNH $20 + $5 /1st copy shipping   ____ _____

Circle of Friends   by Bob & Martha Perske $25 + $5 /1st copy shipping   ____ _____

Unequal Justice by Bob Perske	$25 + $5 /1st copy shipping	____	____
Perske - Pencil Portraits 1971-1990	$30 + $5 /1st copy shipping	____	____
Inclusion – Exclusion Poster (18 X 24)	$10 + $5 /1st copy shipping	____	____
Inclusion News (free with book order)			
Inclusion News in Bulk (box of 100)	$50 – includes shipping in NA	____	____

Videos & CD-ROM

TOOLS FOR CHANGE - The CD-Rom for Person Centred Planning   ____

Pricing is dependent on a licensing agreement. To obtain licensing information check our website, e-mail or call us.

ReDiscovering MAPS Charting Your Journey -brand NEW MAPS training video	$100 + $8 shipping /1st copy	____	____
PATH IN ACTION Working with Groups -Training Video for Path with Groups	$100 + $8 shipping /1st copy	____	____
PATH TRAINING Video Intro Training Video - An Individual Path {Joe's Path}	$75 + $8 shipping /1st copy	____	____
PATH Demo Video Univ of Dayton Ohio - Video of Workshop on PATH	$55 + $8 shipping /1st copy	____	____
Celebrating Marsha (32 minutes of edited clips from Oct.7,2001)	$50 + $8 shipping /1st copy	____	____
Each Belongs (30 years of Inclusion-15 min. celebration in Hamilton)	$50 + $8 shipping /1st copy	____	____
All Means All - Inclusion Video Introduction to Circles, MAPS and PATH	$100 + $8 shipping /1st copy	____	____
When Spider Webs Unite – Video Shafik Asante in Action	$75 + $8 /1st copy shipping	____	____
EVERYONE Has a GIFT John McKnight - Building Communities of Capacity	$75 + $8 shipping /1st copy	____	____
NEW MAPS TRAINING Video Shafik's MAP - MAPS Process - Step by Step	$75 + $8 shipping /1st copy	____	____
Friendship Video Judith, Marsha & Jack on Friendship	$55 + $8 shipping /1st copy	____	____
Petroglyphs Video - the High School video -	$55 + $8 shipping /1st copy	____	____
Companionto/images from the Petroglyphs Book - **Packaged with book - $60 + $8 shipping**			
Dream Catchers (Dreams & Circles)	$55 + $8 shipping /1st copy	____	____
Miller's MAP - MAPS in Action	$55 + $8 shipping /1st copy	____	____
With a Little Help from My Friends The Classic on Circles & MAPS	$55 + $8 shipping /1st copy	____	____
Kids Belong Together - MAPS & Circles	$55 + $8 shipping /1st copy	____	____
Together We're Better (3 videos) Staff Development Kit	$175 + $12 shipping	____	____

Cheques, Money Orders, Purchase Orders Please.
* **Prices subject to change without notice. Shipping prices for North America only. Elsewhere by quote.**

---

* Shipping: Books: $5 for 1st + $2/copy; Videos: $8 for 1st+ $4/copy. OR 15% of total order cost - which ever is less for customer.

Plus applicable taxes (variable)

GRAND TOTAL $===========

Tools for Change – the CD
Tools for Person Centred Planning

Name:	_____
Organization:	_____
Address:	_____
City:	_____
Prov./State _____	Post Code/ZIP _____
Work Phone _____	Cheque Enclosed _____
Home Phone _____	Fax _____
E-Mail _____	Web Page: _____

INCLUSION PRESS ORDER FORM

24 Thome Crescent, Toronto, ON Canada M6H 2S5
Tel: 416-658-5363 Fax: 416-658-5067
E-mail: inclusionpress@inclusion.com
WEBSITE: http://www.inclusion.com

Inclusion SPECIAL PACKS...

* PATH IN ACTION PACK — $150 + $15 shipping/pack ____ _____
- 2 Path Training Videos [(Path in Action + Path Training) + Path Workbook]

* All Means All PACK — $110 + $10 shipping/pack ____ _____
- Video: All Means All, plus & book: All My Life's a Circle

* Friendship PACK (1 book + Video) — $ 60 + $10 shipping/pack ____ _____
- [Friendship Video + From Behind the Piano/What's Really Worth Doing]

* Inclusion Classics Videos PACK — $ 90 + $12 shipping/pack ____ _____
- Videos [With a Little Help from My Friends + Kids Belong Together]

* Inclusion Classics Book PACK — $ 30 + $7 shipping/pack ____ _____
- Books [Action for Inclusion + The Inclusion Papers]

* Petroglyphs PACK — $ 60 + $10 shipping/pack ____ _____
- Petroglyphs Book and Video on Inclusion in High Schools - from UNH

* When Spider Webs Unite PACK — $ 80 + $10 shipping/pack ____ _____
- When Spider Webs Unite - Shafik Asante - Book and Video

* The Education Book PACK — $ 40 + $7 shipping/pack ____ _____
- Inclusion: Recent Research & Inclusion: How To - 2 Books - Gary Bunch

* The Community PACK — $ 40 + $7 shipping/pack ____ _____
- Members of Each Other & Celebrating the Ordinary - 2 books - John O'Brien & Connie Lyle O'Brien

Books

Books	Copies Total
A Little Book About Person Centered Planning	$20 + $5 /1st copy shipping ____ _____
Edited by John O'Brien & Connie Lyle O'Brien with Forest, Lovett, Mount, Pearpoint, Smull, Snow, and Strully	
All My Life's a Circle Expanded Edition- Circles, MAPS & PATH	$20 + $5 /1st copy shipping ____ _____
Path Workbook - 2nd Edition Planning Positive Possible Futures	$20 + $5 /1st copy shipping ____ _____
Celebrating the Ordinary O'Brien, O'Brien & Jacob	$25 + $5 /1st copy shipping ____ _____
Members of Each Other John O'Brien & Connie Lyle O'Brien	$25 + $5 /1st copy shipping ____ _____
Action for Inclusion - Classic on Inclusion	$20 + $5 /1st copy shipping ____ _____
The Inclusion Papers - Strategies & Stories	$20 + $5 /1st copy shipping ____ _____
Lessons for Inclusion Curriculum Ideas for Inclusion in Elementary Schools	$20 + $5 /1st copy shipping ____ _____
Inclusion: How To Essential Classroom Strategies - Gary Bunch	$25+ $5 /1st copy shipping ____ _____
Inclusion: Recent Research G. Bunch & A. Valeo	$25 + $5 /1st copy shipping ____ _____
Kids, Disabilities Regular Classrooms Gary Bunch	$20 + $5 /1st copy shipping ____ _____
Reflections on Inclusive Education	$15 + $5 /1st copy shipping ____ _____
Each Belongs - Hamilton Wentworth Catholic School Bd - J. Hansen	$20 + $5 /1st copy shipping ____ _____
From Behind the Piano, by Jack Pearpoint AND **What's Really Worth Doing** by Judith Snow - Now in ONE Book *	$20 + $5 /1st copy shipping ____ _____
When Spider Webs Unite Community & Inclusion- Shafik Asante	$20 + $5 /1st copy shipping ____ _____
Yes! She Knows She's Here Nicola Schaefer's NEW Book	$20 + $5 /1st copy shipping ____ _____
Dream Catchers & Dolphins Marsha Forest and Jack Pearpoint	$20 + $5 /1st copy shipping ____ _____
It Matters - Lessons from my Son - Janice Fialka	$15 + $5 /1st copy shipping ____ _____
Do You Hear What I Hear? - Janice Fialka & Karen Mikus	$15 + $5 /1st copy shipping ____ _____
The Careless Society - John McKnight	$25 + $5 /1st copy shipping ____ _____
Who Cares - David Schwartz	$30 + $5 /1st copy shipping ____ _____
The All Star Company - Team Building by Nick Marsh	$20 + $5 /1st copy shipping ____ _____
Changes in Latitudes/Attitudes Role of the Inclusion Facilitator	$20 + $5 /1st copy shipping ____ _____
Petroglyphs - Inclusion in High School from UNH	$20 + $5 /1st copy shipping ____ _____
Treasures - from UNH	$20 + $5 /1st copy shipping ____ _____
Circle of Friends by Bob & Martha Perske	$25 + $5 /1st copy shipping ____ _____

Unequal Justice by Bob Perske	$25 + $5 /1st copy shipping	____	____
Perske - Pencil Portraits 1971-1990	$30 + $5 /1st copy shipping	____	____
Inclusion – Exclusion Poster (18 X 24)	$10 + $5 /1st copy shipping	____	____
Inclusion News (free with book order)		____	____
Inclusion News in Bulk (box of 100)	$50 – includes shipping in NA	____	____

Videos & CD-ROM

TOOLS FOR CHANGE - The CD-Rom for Person Centred Planning   ____

Pricing is dependent on a licensing agreement. To obtain licensing information check our website, e-mail or call us.

ReDiscovering MAPS Charting Your Journey -brand NEW MAPS training video	$100 + $8 shipping /1st copy	____	____
PATH IN ACTION Working with Groups -Training Video for Path with Groups	$100 + $8 shipping /1st copy	____	____
PATH TRAINING Video Intro Training Video - An Individual Path {Joe's Path}	$75 + $8 shipping /1st copy	____	____
PATH Demo Video Univ of Dayton Ohio - Video of Workshop on PATH	$55 + $8 shipping /1st copy	____	____
Celebrating Marsha (32 minutes of edited clips from Oct.7,2001)	$50 + $8 shipping /1st copy	____	____
Each Belongs (30 years of Inclusion-15 min. celebration in Hamilton)	$50 + $8 shipping /1st copy	____	____
All Means All - Inclusion Video Introduction to Circles, MAPS and PATH	$100 + $8 shipping /1st copy	____	____
When Spider Webs Unite - Video Shafik Asante in Action	$75 + $8 /1st copy shipping	____	____
EVERYONE Has a GIFT John McKnight - Building Communities of Capacity	$75 + $8 shipping /1st copy	____	____
NEW MAPS TRAINING Video Shafik's MAP - MAPS Process - Step by Step	$75 + $8 shipping /1st copy	____	____
Friendship Video Judith, Marsha & Jack on Friendship	$55 + $8 shipping /1st copy	____	____
Petroglyphs Video - the High School video -	$55 + $8 shipping /1st copy	____	____
Companionto/images from the Petroglyphs Book - Packaged with book - $60 + $8 shipping			
Dream Catchers (Dreams & Circles)	$55 + $8 shipping /1st copy	____	____
Miller's MAP - MAPS in Action	$55 + $8 shipping /1st copy	____	____
With a Little Help from My Friends The Classic on Circles & MAPS	$55 + $8 shipping /1st copy	____	____
Kids Belong Together - MAPS & Circles	$55 + $8 shipping /1st copy	____	____
Together We're Better (3 videos) Staff Development Kit	$175 + $12 shipping	____	____

*Cheques, Money Orders, Purchase Orders
Please.*
* Prices subject to change without notice.
Shipping prices for North America only.
Elsewhere by quote.
_____
* Shipping: Books: $5 for 1st + $2/copy;
Videos: $8 for 1st+ $4/copy. OR 15% of total
order cost - which ever is less for customer.

Plus applicable taxes (variable)

GRAND TOTAL $===========

Tools for Change – the CD
Tools for Person Centred Planning

Name:	_____
Organization:	_____
Address:	_____
City:	_____
Prov./State	_____ Post Code/ZIP _____
Work Phone	_____ Cheque Enclosed _____
Home Phone	_____ Fax _____
E-Mail	_____ Web Page: _____

INCLUSION PRESS ORDER FORM

24 Thorne Crescent, Toronto, ON Canada M6H 2S5
Tel: 416-658-5363 Fax: 416-658-5067
E-mail: inclusionpress@inclusion.com
WEBSITE: http://www.inclusion.com

Inclusion SPECIAL PACKS...

* PATH IN ACTION PACK $150 + $15 shipping/pack   ____ _____
- 2 Path Training Videos [(Path in Action + Path Training) + Path Workbook]

* All Means All PACK $110 + $10 shipping/pack   ____ _____
- Video: All Means All, plus & book: All My Life's a Circle

* Friendship PACK (1 book + Video) $ 60 + $10 shipping/pack   ____ _____
- [Friendship Video + From Behind the Piano/What's Really Worth Doing]

* Inclusion Classics Videos PACK $ 90 + $12 shipping/pack   ____ _____
- Videos [With a Little Help from My Friends + Kids Belong Together]

* Inclusion Classics Book PACK $ 30 + $7 shipping/pack   ____ _____
- Books [Action for Inclusion + The Inclusion Papers]

* Petroglyphs PACK $ 60 + $10 shipping/pack   ____ _____
- Petroglyphs Book and Video on Inclusion in High Schools - from UNH

* When Spider Webs Unite PACK $ 80 + $10 shipping/pack   ____ _____
- When Spider Webs Unite - Shafik Asante - Book and Video

* The Education Book PACK $ 40 + $7 shipping/pack   ____ _____
- Inclusion: Recent Research & Inclusion: How To - 2 Books - Gary Bunch

* The Community PACK $ 40 + $7 shipping/pack   ____ _____
- Members of Each Other & Celebrating the Ordinary - 2 books - John O'Brien & Connie Lyle O'Brien

Books	Copies Total
A Little Book About Person Centered Planning	$20 + $5 /1st copy shipping ____ ____
Edited by John O'Brien & Connie Lyle O'Brien with Forest, Lovett, Mount, Pearpoint, Smull, Snow, and Strully	
All My Life's a Circle Expanded Edition- Circles, MAPS & PATH	$20 + $5 /1st copy shipping ____ ____
Path Workbook - 2nd Edition Planning Positive Possible Futures	$20 + $5 /1st copy shipping ____ ____
Celebrating the Ordinary O'Brien, O'Brien & Jacob	$25 + $5 /1st copy shipping ____ ____
Members of Each Other John O'Brien & Connie Lyle O'Brien	$25 + $5 /1st copy shipping ____ ____
Action for Inclusion - Classic on Inclusion	$20 + $5 /1st copy shipping ____ ____
The Inclusion Papers - Strategies & Stories	$20 + $5 /1st copy shipping ____ ____
Lessons for Inclusion Curriculum Ideas for Inclusion in Elementary Schools	$20 + $5 /1st copy shipping ____ ____
Inclusion: How To Essential Classroom Strategies - Gary Bunch	$25+ $5 /1st copy shipping ____ ____
Inclusion: Recent Research G. Bunch & A. Valeo	$25 + $5 /1st copy shipping ____ ____
Kids, Disabilities Regular Classrooms Gary Bunch	$20 + $5 /1st copy shipping ____ ____
Reflections on Inclusive Education	$15 + $5 /1st copy shipping ____ ____
Each Belongs - Hamilton Wentworth Catholic School Bd - J. Hansen	$20 + $5 /1st copy shipping ____ ____
From Behind the Piano, by Jack Pearpoint AND **What's Really Worth Doing** by Judith Snow - Now in ONE Book *	$20 + $5 /1st copy shipping ____ ____
When Spider Webs Unite Community & Inclusion- Shafik Asante	$20 + $5 /1st copy shipping ____ ____
Yes! She Knows She's Here Nicola Schaefer's NEW Book	$20 + $5 /1st copy shipping ____ ____
Dream Catchers & Dolphins Marsha Forest and Jack Pearpoint	$20 + $5 /1st copy shipping ____ ____
It Matters - Lessons from my Son - Janice Fialka	$15 + $5 /1st copy shipping ____ ____
Do You Hear What I Hear? - Janice Fialka & Karen Mikus	$15 + $5 /1st copy shipping ____ ____
The Careless Society - John McKnight	$25 + $5 /1st copy shipping ____ ____
Who Cares - David Schwartz	$30 + $5 /1st copy shipping ____ ____
The All Star Company - Team Building by Nick Marsh	$20 + $5 /1st copy shipping ____ ____
Changes in Latitudes/Attitudes Role of the Inclusion Facilitator	$20 + $5 /1st copy shipping ____ ____
Petroglyphs - Inclusion in High School from UNH	$20 + $5 /1st copy shipping ____ ____
Treasures - from UNH	$20 + $5 /1st copy shipping ____ ____
Circle of Friends by Bob & Martha Perske	$25 + $5 /1st copy shipping ____ ____

Unequal Justice by Bob Perske	$25 + $5 /1st copy shipping	_____ _____
Perske - Pencil Portraits 1971-1990	$30 + $5 /1st copy shipping	_____ _____
Inclusion – Exclusion Poster (18 X 24)	$10 + $5 /1st copy shipping	_____ _____
Inclusion News (free with book order)		_____ _____
Inclusion News in Bulk (box of 100)	$50 – includes shipping in NA	_____ _____

Videos & CD-ROM

TOOLS FOR CHANGE - The CD-Rom for Person Centred Planning   _____

Pricing is dependent on a licensing agreement. To obtain licensing information check our website, e-mail or call us.

ReDiscovering MAPS Charting Your Journey -brand NEW MAPS training video	$100 + $8 shipping /1st copy	_____ _____
PATH IN ACTION Working with Groups -Training Video for Path with Groups	$100 + $8 shipping /1st copy	_____ _____
PATH TRAINING Video Intro Training Video - An Individual Path {Joe's Path}	$75 + $8 shipping /1st copy	_____ _____
PATH Demo Video Univ of Dayton Ohio - Video of Workshop on PATH	$55 + $8 shipping /1st copy	_____ _____
Celebrating Marsha (32 minutes of edited clips from Oct.7,2001)	$50 + $8 shipping /1st copy	_____ _____
Each Belongs (30 years of Inclusion-15 min. celebration in Hamilton)	$50 + $8 shipping /1st copy	_____ _____
All Means All - Inclusion Video Introduction to Circles, MAPS and PATH	$100 + $8 shipping /1st copy	_____ _____
When Spider Webs Unite - Video Shafik Asante in Action	$75 + $8 /1st copy shipping	_____ _____
EVERYONE Has a GIFT John McKnight - Building Communities of Capacity	$75 + $8 shipping /1st copy	_____ _____
NEW MAPS TRAINING Video Shafik's MAP - MAPS Process - Step by Step	$75 + $8 shipping /1st copy	_____ _____
Friendship Video Judith, Marsha & Jack on Friendship	$55 + $8 shipping /1st copy	_____ _____
Petroglyphs Video - the High School video -	$55 + $8 shipping /1st copy	_____ _____
Companion to/images from the Petroglyphs Book - Packaged with book - $60 + $8 shipping		
Dream Catchers (Dreams & Circles)	$55 + $8 shipping /1st copy	_____ _____
Miller's MAP - MAPS in Action	$55 + $8 shipping /1st copy	_____ _____
With a Little Help from My Friends The Classic on Circles & MAPS	$55 + $8 shipping /1st copy	_____ _____
Kids Belong Together - MAPS & Circles	$55 + $8 shipping /1st copy	_____ _____
Together We're Better (3 videos) Staff Development Kit	$175 + $12 shipping	_____ _____

Cheques, Money Orders, Purchase Orders Please.

* Prices subject to change without notice. Shipping prices for North America only. Elsewhere by quote.

* Shipping: Books: $5 for 1st + $2/copy; Videos: $8 for 1st+ $4/copy. OR 15% of total order cost - which ever is less for customer.

Plus applicable taxes (variable)

GRAND TOTAL $===========

Tools for Change – the CD
Tools for Person Centred Planning

Order NOW: TOOLS for CHANGE CD-ROM

An exciting multi-media Training Guide with resources galore for your staff. Presentation ready. A practical, usable CD-ROM featuring slide shows, graphic overheads, video clips, articles. Introduces 'tools for change' that were developed by Jack Pearpoint, Marsha Forest and John O'Brien. Essential for 'trainers' using Person Centered approaches, MAPS, PATH, Circles or just dealing with day to day change. Includes articles and overheads that can be printed.

Name:	_____
Organization:	_____
Address:	_____
City:	_____
Prov./State	_____ Post Code/ZIP _____
Work Phone	_____ Cheque Enclosed _____
Home Phone	_____ Fax _____
E-Mail	_____ Web Page: _____

Nov. 2001 Listing

INCLUSION PRESS ORDER FORM
24 Thome Crescent, Toronto, ON Canada M6H 2S5
Tel: 416-658-5363 Fax: 416-658-5067
E-mail: inclusionpress@inclusion.com
WEBSITE: http://www.inclusion.com

Inclusion SPECIAL PACKS...

* PATH IN ACTION PACK $150 + $15 shipping/pack   ____ _____
- 2 Path Training Videos [(Path in Action + Path Training) + Path Workbook]

* All Means All PACK $110 + $10 shipping/pack   ____ _____
- Video: All Means All, plus & book: All My Life's a Circle

* Friendship PACK (1 book + Video) $ 60 + $10 shipping/pack   ____ _____
- [Friendship Video + From Behind the Piano/What's Really Worth Doing]

* Inclusion Classics Videos PACK $ 90 + $12 shipping/pack   ____ _____
- Videos [With a Little Help from My Friends + Kids Belong Together]

* Inclusion Classics Book PACK $ 30 + $7 shipping/pack   ____ _____
- Books [Action for Inclusion + The Inclusion Papers]

* Petroglyphs PACK $ 60 + $10 shipping/pack   ____ _____
- Petroglyphs Book and Video on Inclusion in High Schools - from UNH

* When Spider Webs Unite PACK $ 80 + $10 shipping/pack   ____ _____
- When Spider Webs Unite - Shafik Asante - Book and Video

* The Education Book PACK $ 40 + $7 shipping/pack   ____ _____
- Inclusion: Recent Research & Inclusion: How To - 2 Books - Gary Bunch

* The Community PACK $ 40 + $7 shipping/pack   ____ _____
- Members of Each Other & Celebrating the Ordinary - 2 books - John O'Brien & Connie Lyle O'Brien

Books	Copies Total		
A Little Book About Person Centered Planning	$20 + $5 /1st copy shipping	____	_____
Edited by John O'Brien & Connie Lyle O'Brien with Forest, Lovett, Mount, Pearpoint, Smull, Snow, and Strully			
All My Life's a Circle Expanded Edition- Circles, MAPS & PATH	$20 + $5 /1st copy shipping	____	_____
Path Workbook - 2nd Edition Planning Positive Possible Futures	$20 + $5 /1st copy shipping	____	_____
Celebrating the Ordinary O'Brien, O'Brien & Jacob	$25 + $5 /1st copy shipping	____	_____
Members of Each Other John O'Brien & Connie Lyle O'Brien	$25 + $5 /1st copy shipping	____	_____
Action for Inclusion - Classic on Inclusion	$20 + $5 /1st copy shipping	____	_____
The Inclusion Papers - Strategies & Stories	$20 + $5 /1st copy shipping	____	_____
Lessons for Inclusion Curriculum Ideas for Inclusion in Elementary Schools	$20 + $5 /1st copy shipping	____	_____
Inclusion: How To Essential Classroom Strategies - Gary Bunch	$25+ $5 /1st copy shipping	____	_____
Inclusion: Recent Research G. Bunch & A. Valeo	$25 + $5 /1st copy shipping	____	_____
Kids, Disabilities Regular Classrooms Gary Bunch	$20 + $5 /1st copy shipping	____	_____
Reflections on Inclusive Education	$15 + $5 /1st copy shipping	____	_____
Each Belongs - Hamilton Wentworth Catholic School Bd - J. Hansen	$20 + $5 /1st copy shipping	____	_____
From Behind the Piano, by Jack Pearpoint AND **What's Really Worth Doing** by Judith Snow - Now in ONE Book *	$20 + $5 /1st copy shipping	____	_____
When Spider Webs Unite Community & Inclusion- Shafik Asante	$20 + $5 /1st copy shipping	____	_____
Yes! She Knows She's Here Nicola Schaefer's NEW Book	$20 + $5 /1st copy shipping	____	_____
Dream Catchers & Dolphins Marsha Forest and Jack Pearpoint	$20 + $5 /1st copy shipping	____	_____
It Matters - Lessons from my Son - Janice Fialka	$15 + $5 /1st copy shipping	____	_____
Do You Hear What I Hear? - Janice Fialka & Karen Mikus	$15 + $5 /1st copy shipping	____	_____
The Careless Society - John McKnight	$25 + $5 /1st copy shipping	____	_____
Who Cares - David Schwartz	$30 + $5 /1st copy shipping	____	_____
The All Star Company - Team Building by Nick Marsh	$20 + $5 /1st copy shipping	____	_____
Changes in Latitudes/Attitudes Role of the Inclusion Facilitator	$20 + $5 /1st copy shipping	____	_____
Petroglyphs - Inclusion in High School from UNH	$20 + $5 /1st copy shipping	____	_____
Treasures - from UNH	$20 + $5 /1st copy shipping	____	_____
Circle of Friends by Bob & Martha Perske	$25 + $5 /1st copy shipping	____	_____

Unequal Justice by Bob Perske	$25 + $5 /1st copy shipping	____	____
Perske - Pencil Portraits 1971-1990	$30 + $5 /1st copy shipping	____	____
Inclusion – Exclusion Poster (18 X 24)	$10 + $5 /1st copy shipping		
Inclusion News (free with book order)		____	____
Inclusion News in Bulk (box of 100)	$50 – includes shipping in NA	____	____

Videos & CD-ROM

TOOLS FOR CHANGE - The CD-Rom for Person Centred Planning ____

Pricing is dependent on a licensing agreement. To obtain licensing information check our website, e-mail or call us.

ReDiscovering MAPS Charting Your Journey -brand NEW MAPS training video	$100 + $8 shipping /1st copy	____	____
PATH IN ACTION Working with Groups -Training Video for Path with Groups	$100 + $8 shipping /1st copy	____	____
PATH TRAINING Video Intro Training Video - An Individual Path {Joe's Path}	$75 + $8 shipping /1st copy	____	____
PATH Demo Video Univ of Dayton Ohio - Video of Workshop on PATH	$55 + $8 shipping /1st copy	____	____
Celebrating Marsha (32 minutes of edited clips from Oct.7,2001)	$50 + $8 shipping /1st copy	____	____
Each Belongs (30 years of Inclusion-15 min. celebration in Hamilton)	$50 + $8 shipping /1st copy	____	____
All Means All - Inclusion Video Introduction to Circles, MAPS and PATH	$100 + $8 shipping /1st copy	____	____
When Spider Webs Unite - Video Shafik Asante in Action	$75 + $8 /1st copy shipping	____	____
EVERYONE Has a GIFT John McKnight - Building Communities of Capacity	$75 + $8 shipping /1st copy	____	____
NEW MAPS TRAINING Video Shafik's MAP - MAPS Process - Step by Step	$75 + $8 shipping /1st copy	____	____
Friendship Video Judith, Marsha & Jack on Friendship	$55 + $8 shipping /1st copy	____	____
Petroglyphs Video - the High School video -	$55 + $8 shipping /1st copy	____	____
Companionto/images from the Petroglyphs Book - Packaged with book - $60 + $8 shipping			
Dream Catchers (Dreams & Circles)	$55 + $8 shipping /1st copy	____	____
Miller's MAP - MAPS in Action	$55 + $8 shipping /1st copy	____	____
With a Little Help from My Friends The Classic on Circles & MAPS	$55 + $8 shipping /1st copy	____	____
Kids Belong Together - MAPS & Circles	$55 + $8 shipping /1st copy	____	____
Together We're Better (3 videos) Staff Development Kit	$175 + $12 shipping	____	____

Cheques, Money Orders, Purchase Orders Please.

Plus applicable taxes (variable)

* Prices subject to change without notice. Shipping prices for North America only. Elsewhere by quote.

GRAND TOTAL $===========

---

* Shipping: Books: $5 for 1st + $2/copy; Videos: $8 for 1st+ $4/copy. OR 15% of total order cost - which ever is less for customer.

Tools for Change – the CD
Tools for Person Centred Planning

Order NOW: TOOLS for CHANGE CD-ROM

An exciting multi-media Training Guide with resources galore for your staff. Presentation ready. A practical, usable CD-ROM featuring slide shows, graphic overheads, video clips, articles. Introduces 'tools for change' that were developed by Jack Pearpoint, Marsha Forest and John O'Brien. Essential for 'trainers' using Person Centered approaches, MAPS, PATH, Circles or just dealing with day to day change. Includes articles and overheads that can be printed.

Name:	_____
Organization:	_____
Address:	_____
City:	_____
Prov./State	_____ Post Code/ZIP _____
Work Phone	_____ Cheque Enclosed _____
Home Phone	_____ Fax _____
E-Mail	_____ Web Page: _____